WELCOME!

On behalf of Splash! Publications, we would like to welcome you to *Spanish Explorers and Conquistadors*, one of several books in our American History series. Since this curriculum was designed by teachers, we are positive that you will find it to be the most comprehensive program you have ever utilized to teach students about some of our earliest explorers. We would like to take a few moments to familiarize you with the program.

THE FORMAT

Spanish Explorers and Conquistadors is a twelve lesson program. Our goal is a curriculum that you can use the very first day you purchase our materials. No lessons to plan, comprehension questions to write, activities to create, or vocabulary words to define. Simply open the book and start teaching.

Each of the twelve lessons requires students to complete vocabulary cards, read about one of the Spanish explorers or conquistadors, and complete a comprehension activity that will expose them to various standardized test formats. In addition, each lesson includes a balanced mix of lower and higher level activities for students to complete. Vocabulary quizzes, mapping activities that teach cardinal directions and latitude/longitude, grid math, thought provoking discussion questions, research projects utilizing primary and secondary sources, graphic organizers for story writing and journaling, time lines, and following directions are the types of activities that will guide students through their journey of *Spanish Explorers and Conquistadors*.

THE LESSON PLANS

On the next several pages, you will find the Lesson Plans for *Spanish Explorers and Conquistadors*. The Lesson Plans clearly outline what students must do before, during, and after each lesson. Page numbers are listed so that you will immediately know what you need to photocopy before beginning each lesson. The answers to all activities, quizzes, and comprehension questions are located on pages 104-110.

NOTE: Students will complete a culminating activity at the end of the unit. We suggest that students keep the information from each lesson in a notebook or folder.

THE VOCABULARY

Each lesson features words in bold type. We have included a Glossary on pages 98-103 to help students pronounce and define the words. Unlike a dictionary, the definitions in the Glossary are concise and written in context. Remember, we're teachers! Students will be exposed to these vocabulary words in the comprehension activities. They will also be tested on the vocabulary words four times throughout their study of *Spanish Explorers and Conquistadors*.

Students will be responsible for filling out and studying the vocabulary cards. You may want to have students bring in a small box for storing their vocabulary cards. We don't have to tell you that incorporating these words into your Reading and Spelling programs will save time and make the words more meaningful for students.

CORE STANDARDS: THE "BIG IDEAS"

Core Standards help teachers prioritize instruction and connect the "big ideas" students need to know in order to advance. As a reading-based unit, *Spanish Explorers and Conquistadors* fosters literacy in Social Studies.

At the same time that students are learning important factual content about *Spanish Explorers and Conquistadors,* they are meeting the Common Core Standards for English Language Arts and making connections to the "big ideas" in American History. Alignment to the 3rd-5th Grade Common Core Standards is clearly noted in the Lesson Plans. Below is the legend used to abbreviate the Common Core Strands:

COMMON CORE STRAND CODE:
CC = COMMON CORE
RL = READING-LITERATURE
RI = READING INFORMATIONAL TEXT
RF = READING FOUNDATIONS SKILLS
W = WRITING
SL = SPEAKING LISTENING
L = LANGUAGE

THE COPYRIGHT

Illustrations and cover design by Victoria J. Smith

ISBN 978-1-935255-01-7

OUR OTHER TITLES

COMPLETE STATE HISTORY PROGRAMS
Do American History!
Do Arizona!
Do California!
Do Colorado!
Do Florida!
Do Nevada!
Do New Mexico!
Do Texas!
Do Washington!

LITERATURE STUDY GUIDES
Charlotte's Web
Cricket in Times Square
Enormous Egg
Sarah, Plain and Tall

PRIMARY SERIES
Leveled Math: Addition Bk 1
Leveled Math: Addition Bk 2
Leveled Math: Subtraction Bk 1
Leveled Math: Subtraction Bk 2
National Holidays
National Symbols
Poems for Every Holiday
Poems for Every Season

AMERICAN HISTORY SERIES
New World Explorers
The Thirteen Original Colonies
Early American Government
The American Revolution
Slavery in America
The Civil War
Westward Expansion

U.S. REGION SERIES
The Middle Atlantic States
The New England States
The Great Lakes States
The Great Plains States
The Southeast States
The Southwest States
The Mountain States
The Pacific States

STATE HISTORY SERIES
Arizona Geography
Arizona Animals
Arizona History
Arizona Government & Economy
California Geography
California Animals
California History
California Government & Economy
Florida Geography
Florida Animals
Florida History
Florida Government & Economy
Illinois History
Indiana History
Michigan History
Ohio History
Texas Geography
Texas Animals
Texas History
Texas Government & Economy

TABLE OF CONTENTS

SPANISH EXPLORERS AND CONQUISTADORS

TABLE OF CONTENTS

SPANISH EXPLORERS AND CONQUISTADORS (CONTINUED)

LESSONS *at a* GLANCE

1. Before reading Christopher Columbus, students will:
- complete Vocabulary Cards for *accused, appointed, Asia, Caribbean Sea, coast, conquered, continent, convinced, estimated, European, geography, governor, harsh, Hispaniola, historians, ignored, inhabitants, islands, journal, kidnapped, mainland, merchant, native, navigation, New World, North America, Portugal, resources, seaport, strait, stranded, tavern, torture, voyage, West Indies, witnesses. (pg. 1)*

After reading Christopher Columbus *(pps. 2-7)*, students will:
- answer Christopher Columbus Comprehension Questions. *(pg. 8)*
- plot islands, water resources, and important landforms on a map. *(pps. 9-10)*
- take a Vocabulary Quiz for Spanish Explorers and Conquistadors Part I. *(pps. 11-12)*

THE CHRISTOPHER COLUMBUS LESSON IS ALIGNED WITH THESE 3RD-5TH GRADE CORE STANDARDS: CC.RI.1, CC.RI.2, CC.RI.3, CC.RI.4, CC.RI.7, CC.RI.10, CC.RF.3A, CC.RF.4A, CC.RF.4C, CC.L.4A, CC.L.4C, CC.L.6

2. Before reading Amerigo Vespucci, students will:
- complete Vocabulary Cards for *autobiography, biographies, expeditions, malaria, preserved, scholar. (pg. 1)*

After reading Amerigo Vespucci *(pps. 13-14)*, students will:
- answer Amerigo Vespucci Comprehension Questions. *(pg. 15)*
- differentiate between primary and secondary sources. *(pg. 16)*

THE AMERIGO VESPUCCI LESSON IS ALIGNED WITH THESE 3RD-5TH GRADE CORE STANDARDS: CC.RI.1, CC.RI.2, CC.RI.3, CC.RI.4, CC.RI.6, CC.RI.7, CC.RI.10, CC.RF.3A, CC.RF.4A, CC.RF.4C, CC.L.4A, CC.L.4C, CC.L.6

LESSONS *at a* GLANCE

3. Before reading Vasco Núñez de Balboa, students will:
- complete Vocabulary Cards for *abandoned, befriended, beheaded, colony, conquistador, debt, defeated, denied, dominions, fertile, hostile, Isthmus of Panama, loyally, nobleman, raided, respect, treason, worshipped. (pg. 1)*

After reading Vasco Núñez de Balboa *(pps. 17-20)*, students will:
- answer Vasco Núñez de Balboa Comprehension Questions. *(pg. 21)*
- use number and letter pairs to complete Conquistador Grid Math. *(pps. 22-24)*

THE VASCO NÚÑEZ DE BALBOA LESSON IS ALIGNED WITH THESE 3RD-5TH GRADE CORE STANDARDS: CC.RI.1, CC.RI.2, CC.RI.3, CC.RI.4, CC.RI.7, CC.RI.10, CC.RF.3A, CC.RF.4A, CC.RF.4C, CC.L.4A, CC.L.4C, CC.L.6

4. Before reading Juan Ponce de León, students will:
- complete Vocabulary Cards for *external, founded, legend, Muslims, province. (pg. 1)*

After reading Juan Ponce de León *(pps. 25-26)*, students will:
- answer Juan Ponce de León Comprehension Questions. *(pg. 27)*
- take a Vocabulary Quiz for Spanish Explorers and Conquistadors Part II. *(pps. 28-29)*

THE JUAN PONCE DE LEÓN LESSON IS ALIGNED WITH THESE 3RD-5TH GRADE CORE STANDARDS: CC.RI.1, CC.RI.2, CC.RI.3, CC.RI.4, CC.RI.7, CC.RI.10, CC.RF.3A, CC.RF.4A, CC.RF.4C, CC.L.4A, CC.L.4C, CC.L.6

LESSONS *at a* GLANCE

5. Before reading Ferdinand Magellan, students will:
- complete Vocabulary Cards for *bays, channel, citizen, cloves, military, Philippines, porcelain, scurvy, Spice Islands. (pg. 1)*

After reading Ferdinand Magellan *(pps. 30-32)*, students will:
- answer Ferdinand Magellan Comprehension Questions. *(pg. 33)*
- follow written directions to create a three dimensional miniature globe. *(pps. 34-39)*

THE FERDINAND MAGELLAN LESSON IS ALIGNED WITH THESE 3RD-5TH GRADE CORE STANDARDS:
CC.RI.1, CC.RI.2, CC.RI.3, CC.RI.4, CC.RI.7, CC.RI.10, CC.RF.3A, CC.RF.4A, CC.RF.4C, CC.L.4A, CC.L.4C, CC.L.6

6. Before reading Hernando Cortés, students will:
- complete Vocabulary Cards for *agriculture, Barbary Coast, blockade, canals, capital, ceremonies, Christianity, customs, emperor, empire, exiled, expanding, fertilized, import, irrigate, New Spain, officials, pleurisy, ransom, recruit, sacrificed, sculptures, shallow. (pg. 1)*

After reading Hernando Cortés *(pps. 40-42)*, students will:
- answer Hernando Cortés Comprehension Questions. *(pg. 43)*
- use a graphic organizer to write a Spanish Conquistador Story. *(pps. 44-46)*
- take a Vocabulary Quiz for Spanish Explorers and Conquistadors Part III. *(pps. 47-48)*

THE HERNANDO CORTÉS LESSON IS ALIGNED WITH THESE 3RD-5TH GRADE CORE STANDARDS:
CC.RI.1, CC.RI.2, CC.RI.3, CC.RI.4, CC.RI.10, CC.RF.3A, CC.RF.4A, CC.RF.4C, CC.W.3A, CC.W.3B, CC.W.3C, CC.W.3D, CC.W.3E, CC.W.4, CC.W.5, CC.W.8, CC.W.10, CC.L.4A, CC.L.4C, CC.L.6

Lessons *at a* Glance

7. Before reading Francisco Pizarro, students will:
   • complete Vocabulary Cards for *anchor, archaeologists, architects, artisans, captives, cathedral, conflicts, culture, currents, equator, fleet, harvest, invaded, textiles.* *(pg. 1)*

   After reading Francisco Pizarro *(pps. 49-53)*, students will:
   • answer Francisco Pizarro Comprehension Questions. *(pg. 54)*
   • complete Journal Writing activity about the Inca Empire. *(pg. 55)*

THE FRANCISCO PIZARRO LESSON IS ALIGNED WITH THESE 3RD-5TH GRADE CORE STANDARDS:
CC.RI.1, CC.RI.2, CC.RI.3, CC.RI.4, CC.RI.7, CC.RI.10, CC.RF.3A, CC.RF.4A, CC.RF.4C, CC.W.3A, CC.W.3B, CC.W.3C, CC.W.3D, CC.W.3E, CC.W.4, CC.W.10, CC.L.4A, CC.L.4C, CC.L.6

8. Before reading Cabeza de Vaca, students will:
   • complete Vocabulary Cards for *adobe, barrier island, companions, dunes, emerald, endangered, erosion, flint, foreigners, formations, fossils, Hispanic, innocent, maize, mesas, mission, missionary, monument, mourn, petroglyph, plains, provisions, quarries, species, tourist, turquoise.* *(pg. 1)*

   After reading Cabeza de Vaca *(pps. 56-58)*, students will:
   • answer Cabeza de Vaca Comprehension Questions. *(pg. 59)*
   • use cardinal and intermediate directions to plot points of interest on a map. *(pps. 60-64)*
   • take a Vocabulary Quiz for Spanish Explorers and Conquistadors Part IV. *(pps. 65-66)*

THE CABEZA DE VACA LESSON IS ALIGNED WITH THESE 3RD-5TH GRADE CORE STANDARDS:
CC.RI.1, CC.RI.2, CC.RI.3, CC.RI.4, CC.RI.7, CC.RI.10, CC.RF.3A, CC.RF.4A, CC.RF.4C, CC.L.4A, CC.L.4C, CC.L.6

Lessons at a Glance

9. Before reading Hernando de Soto, students will:
- complete Vocabulary Cards for *ambushed, brutality, engineers, Great Lakes, livestock, panhandle, Yucatán Peninsula.* *(pg. 1)*

After reading Hernando de Soto *(pps. 67-70),* students will:
- answer Hernando de Soto Comprehension Questions. *(pg. 71)*
- create a time line for Hernando de Soto in Time Travel Part I. *(pg. 72)*
- create a time line for someone else in Time Travel Part II. *(pg. 73)*

THE HERNANDO DE SOTO LESSON IS ALIGNED WITH THESE 3RD-5TH GRADE CORE STANDARDS: CC.RI.1, CC.RI.2, CC.RI.3, CC.RI.4, CC.RI.6, CC.RI.7, CC.RI.10, CC.RF.3A, CC.RF.4A, CC.RF.4C, CC.L.4A, CC.L.4C, CC.L.6

10. Before reading Francisco de Coronado, students will:
- complete Vocabulary Cards for *artifacts, exhibits, habitats, hoax, investigate, observatory, pioneers, pueblo, rebellion, treasurer.* *(pg. 1)*

After reading Francisco de Coronado *(pps. 74-75),* students will:
- answer Francisco de Coronado Comprehension Questions. *(pg. 76)*
- use latitude and longitude to plot points of interest on a map. *(pps. 77-82)*

THE FRANCISCO DE CORONADO LESSON IS ALIGNED WITH THESE 3RD-5TH GRADE CORE STANDARDS: CC.RI.1, CC.RI.2, CC.RI.3, CC.RI.4, CC.RI.7, CC.RI.10, CC.RF.3A, CC.RF.4A, CC.RF.4C, CC.L.4A, CC.L.4C, CC.L.6

Lessons *at a* Glance

11. Before reading Juan Cabrillo, students will:
- complete Vocabulary Cards for *crossbows, exported, gangrene, harbor, legacy.* (pg. 1)

After reading Juan Rodríguez Cabrillo *(pps. 83-84),* students will:
- answer Juan Cabrillo Comprehension Questions. *(pg. 85)*
- use primary and secondary sources to create the game Find the Fib. *(pps. 86-90)*
- **Note:** You will need to make four copies of page 87 for each student. We've also supplied you with five miniature pictures of each Spanish explorer and conquistador so you can make copies for the students' Find the Fib cards.

THE JUAN CABRILLO LESSON IS ALIGNED WITH THESE 3RD-5TH GRADE CORE STANDARDS:
CC.RI.1, CC.RI.2, CC.RI.3, CC.RI.4, CC.RI.6, CC.RI.7, CC.RI.10, CC.RF.3A, CC.RF.4A, CC.RF.4C, CC.W.7, CC.W.8, CC.L.4A, CC.L.4C, CC.L.6

12. Before reading the Future of New Spain, students will:
- complete Vocabulary Cards for *allies, blacksmithing, construction, defend, drought, extended, independence, New France, revolted, tanning.* (pg. 1)

After reading the Future of New Spain *(pps. 91-93),* students will:
- answer the Future of New Spain Comprehension Questions. *(pg. 94)*
- complete discussion questions for Spanish Missions. *(pg. 95)*
- take a Vocabulary Quiz for Spanish Explorers and Conquistadors Part V. *(pps. 96-97)*

THE FUTURE OF NEW SPAIN LESSON IS ALIGNED WITH THESE 3RD-5TH GRADE CORE STANDARDS:
CC.RI.1, CC.RI.2, CC.RI.3, CC.RI.4, CC.RI.7, CC.RI.10, CC.RF.3A, CC.RF.4A, CC.RF.4C, CC.W.1A, CC.W.1B, CC.W.9B, CC.L.4A, CC.L.4C, CC.L.6

VOCABULARY CARD

word: _____

definition: _____

_____

VOCABULARY CARD

word: _____

definition: _____

_____

VOCABULARY CARD

word: _____

definition: _____

_____

CHRISTOPHER COLUMBUS

Christopher Columbus was born in Genoa, Italy. **Historians** aren't sure of the exact date of his birth, but most agree that it was sometime between August and October of 1451.

As a child, Christopher helped his father Domenico weave wool and run the family's cheese stand. Little is known about Christopher's education, but we do know that he spoke several languages, studied **geography**, and enjoyed reading.

CHRISTOPHER COLUMBUS

COLUMBUS'S LOVE OF THE SEA

In 1470, Domenico moved his wife and children to the **seaport** town of Savona. Dominico bought a **tavern**. Christopher wasn't interested in becoming a **merchant** or serving food and drinks to customers. His love was the sea.

By 1476, Columbus was working on a ship off the **coast** of **Portugal** (POR•chuw•gal). The ship was attacked by French pirates. Columbus and the rest of the crew were thrown overboard. Nineteen year old Christopher survived by swimming six miles back to shore.

Christopher's brother owned a book and map store nearby in the Portuguese city of Lisbon. Columbus traveled to Lisbon and began working with his brother. Within a few years, Columbus had taught himself everything he could about **navigation** and mapmaking.

FINDING A ROUTE TO ASIA

Columbus became especially interested in learning about Italian explorer Marco Polo. Almost two hundred years before Christopher Columbus was born, Marco Polo had traveled to **Asia**. Making the journey to Asia was very important for Marco Polo and other **European** explorers. In Asia, they could buy jewels, silk, and spices not available in Europe. The only way to get these items was to buy them from Italian traders. The Italian traders purchased the items in Asia and sold them at very high prices to Europeans. If explorers found a water route to Asia, they could buy the things they wanted without paying the Italian traders anything.

Marco Polo traveled over land to Asia. He left from Italy and sailed through the Mediterranean Sea before crossing the mountains and deserts of Asia, known as the Silk Road. Marco Polo's journey lasted 24 years, but he made it to China.

Other explorers searched for an eastward water route to Asia. They sailed around the tip of Africa. Violent storms in this part of the Atlantic Ocean made this route very dangerous.

Christopher Columbus believed that by sailing west, he could find a shorter and safer route to Asia. He **estimated** that Asia was just 3,000 miles west of Europe. He did not know, of course, that the **continent** of **North America** stood in his way. Asia was actually 10,000 miles west of Europe!

- - - - MARCO POLO'S ROUTE TO ASIA

———— OTHER ROUTES TO ASIA

COLUMBUS'S VOYAGE TO THE NEW WORLD

Beginning in 1484, Christopher Columbus begged the leaders of Portugal to pay for a trip across the Atlantic Ocean. They refused to give him money. A year later, Columbus traveled to Spain. He asked King Ferdinand and Queen Isabella to help him. It took six long years, but Queen Isabella finally agreed to support Columbus's plan of sailing west toward Asia. She gave him enough money for ships and supplies.

On August 3, 1492, Christopher Columbus and a crew of 90 men and boys set sail on three small ships named the *Niña*, the *Pinta*, and the *Santa Maria*. They headed westward to find the East Indies in Asia.

After more than a month of sailing, Columbus and his crew sighted a group of **islands**. Columbus thought they had reached the East Indies in Asia. Actually, they had only sailed to the islands just south of Florida in the **Caribbean Sea**. These islands are known today as the **West Indies**.

Historians believe Christopher Columbus first landed on an island in the Bahamas that he named San Salvador. Columbus claimed the entire area for Spain. He explored the islands looking for the riches that Marco Polo had written about. He thought he was in the East Indies of Asia, so he named the strange people he met Indians.

There were more than 40,000 Indians living in the West Indies when Columbus arrived. Since these people were the first **inhabitants** of America, we call them Native Americans today. Columbus wrote in his **journal** that he thought the Indians would make good slaves. They didn't seem to have any religion of their own and he believed they could easily be **conquered** with about 50 men. Columbus planned to take six Indians back to Spain with him.

- - - - **CHRISTOPHER COLUMBUS'S ROUTE TO "ASIA"**

LA NAVIDAD

In the West Indies, Columbus explored the northeast coast of present-day Cuba and the northern coast of **Hispaniola** (his•pan•ee•OH•luh). Before returning to Spain, the **native** people helped him build a fort on Hispaniola. He left 39 of his men at the fort that he named La Navidad, which meant Christmas in English. Instead of taking just six Indians with him, Columbus **kidnapped** about 25 of them. Only seven survived the journey back to Spain.

In the spring of 1493, Christopher Columbus arrived in Spain. Since he did not bring back spices or other Asian products, many doubted that he had actually been to Asia. Explorers still believed that the best route to Asia could be found by sailing around the tip of Africa. Still, King Ferdinand and Queen Isabella **appointed** Columbus as **governor** of the West Indies. They agreed to pay for a second **voyage**.

COLUMBUS'S SECOND VOYAGE

On September 24, 1493, Columbus left Spain with 17 ships carrying supplies and more than 1,000 men. On his way back to the West Indies, Columbus explored and named many of the islands in the Caribbean including present-day Dominica, Antigua, Saint Kitts, Saint Martin, the Virgin Islands, and Puerto Rico.

On November 22, Christopher Columbus arrived in Hispaniola. He found that La Navidad had been destroyed. All of the men had been killed by Native Americans. Columbus quickly established another settlement that he named La Isabella in honor of Queen Isabella. The settlers at La Isabella were promised that they would find gold and silver near La Isabella. Although it only lasted a few years, most historians agree that La Isabella was the first permanent settlement in the **New World**.

On April 24, 1494, Columbus left Hispaniola. He arrived in Cuba six days later. He explored Cuba's southern coast and several nearby islands. On May 5, 1494, Columbus reached Jamaica. He sailed back toward Hispaniola before returning to Spain.

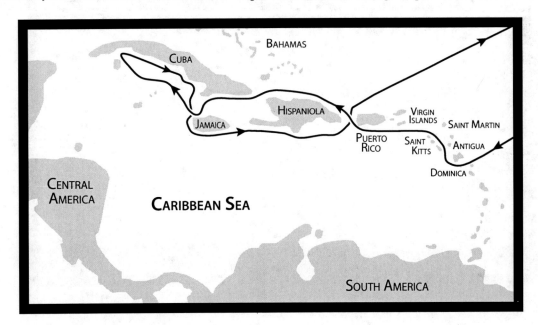

COLUMBUS'S THIRD VOYAGE

On May 30, 1498, Christopher Columbus set sail on his third voyage. He explored and claimed for Spain the **mainland** of South America, and the islands of Trinidad, Margarita, Tobago, and Grenada.

On August 19, 1498, Columbus returned to Hispaniola and the settlement at La Isabella. He wrote in his journal that Hispaniola would be a perfect place to capture Indians to sell as slaves. At La Isabella, Columbus found many angry settlers who **accused** him of being a bad governor. He had some of his crew hanged for disobeying him.

When he returned to Spain, Columbus and his two brothers were arrested. Chains were placed on their arms and legs. During their trial, **witnesses** claimed that Governor Columbus and his brothers had been unfair leaders. They were accused of using **torture** and other **harsh** punishments to gain power in Hispaniola.

After six weeks in jail, King Ferdinand and Queen Isabella ordered the release of Columbus and his brothers. They were given their freedom. Columbus even **convinced** King Ferdinand and Queen Isabella to pay for a fourth voyage. He was, however, replaced by Francisco de Bobadilla (baw•vah•THEE•yah) as governor of the West Indies.

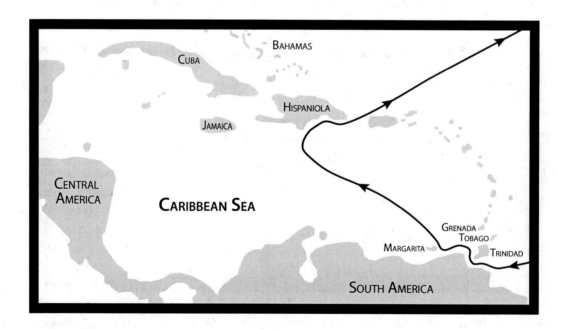

COLUMBUS'S FOURTH VOYAGE

On May 11, 1502, Christopher Columbus left Spain with four ships, his brother Bartolomeo (bar•tol•luh•MAY•yoh), and his 13 year old son, Fernando. A month later, he arrived on the island of Martinique (mar•teh•NEEK). He sailed on toward Hispaniola, hoping to find shelter from a hurricane that was approaching. Governor Bobadilla refused to allow Columbus's ships to land on Hispaniola. The governor also **ignored** Columbus's warning about a hurricane. Columbus sailed on and found shelter near another island.

On July 1, 1502, the hurricane destroyed 29 Spanish ships and killed more than 500 people, including Governor Bobadilla. Columbus's ships survived the storm. He sailed first to Jamaica and then on to Central America. He landed in the Bay Islands off the coast of Honduras. Columbus spent two months exploring the Central American coasts of Honduras, Nicaragua, and Costa Rica. He sailed to Panama where he heard stories of gold and a **strait** to another ocean. Attacks from Native Americans damaged Columbus's ships and forced him to leave Panama before he could search for the gold and the mysterious ocean.

On April 16, 1503, Columbus set sail for Hispaniola. A month later, he sighted the Cayman Islands. He named them Las Tortugas because of all the sea turtles he found there. Another storm damaged his ships, forcing him to land in Jamaica. Columbus and his crew were **stranded** on Jamaica for almost a year. After being rescued, Columbus sailed back to Spain.

Three years later, at the age of 55, Christopher Columbus died. He truly believed he had found some unknown region of Asia. As other explorers made the journey across the Atlantic Ocean, it became clear that Columbus had not discovered a shorter route to Asia. Instead, he had found new lands completely unknown to Europeans.

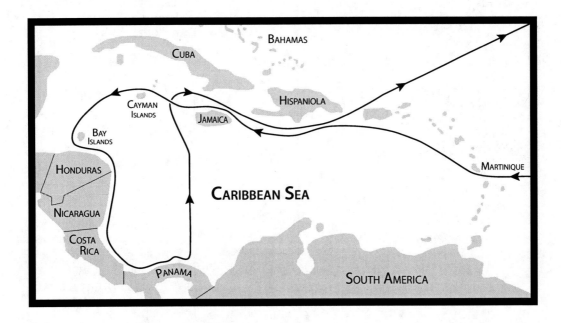

∼∼∼∼∼ CHRISTOPHER COLUMBUS ∼∼∼∼∼

Directions: Read each question carefully. Darken the circle for the correct answer.

1 **Where was Christopher Columbus born?**

   A Spain
   B France
   C Italy
   D Portugal

2 **Why wasn't Christopher Columbus interested in becoming a merchant like his father?**

   F Columbus didn't like working with his father.
   G He wanted to be an astronaut.
   H His love was the sea.
   J He wanted to own a book store with his brother.

3 **What can you learn by studying the map of Marco Polo's route to Asia?**

   A Asia is northeast of Europe.
   B North America is north of Greenland.
   C Marco Polo sailed around the tip of South America.
   D Europe is south of Australia.

4 **Which country gave Christopher Columbus money for his voyage to Asia?**

   F Spain
   G France
   H Italy
   J Portugal

5 **After reading about Columbus's second voyage, you get the idea that –**

   A he took less men and ships than he did on his first voyage
   B he sailed straight to Hispaniola without making any stops
   C his settlement had done very well without him
   D the Native Americans were not as easy to conquer as Christopher Columbus first thought

6 **Why were Christopher Columbus and his brothers arrested?**

   F They had stolen money from Queen Isabella.
   G They were accused of being bad leaders.
   H They had sailed to South America without permission.
   J They wanted to capture Indians to sell as slaves.

7 **How did Christopher Columbus try to save Governor Bobadilla's life?**

   A He rescued Bobadilla from Native Americans.
   B He delivered food and supplies to Hispaniola.
   C He warned the governor about a hurricane.
   D He gave Governor Bobadilla medicine for his wounded leg.

READING

Answers

1 Ⓐ Ⓑ Ⓒ Ⓓ   5 Ⓐ Ⓑ Ⓒ Ⓓ
2 Ⓕ Ⓖ Ⓗ Ⓙ   6 Ⓕ Ⓖ Ⓗ Ⓙ
3 Ⓐ Ⓑ Ⓒ Ⓓ   7 Ⓐ Ⓑ Ⓒ Ⓓ
4 Ⓕ Ⓖ Ⓗ Ⓙ

MAPPING: ISLANDS, WATER RESOURCES, AND LANDFORMS

You have just finished reading about Christopher Columbus's voyages to the New World. During his voyages, Columbus named many of the islands in the Caribbean Sea.

In this activity, you will label many of these islands, water **resources**, and other important landforms and on a blank map.

Directions:

Using the blank map on the next page and your information about Christopher Columbus, correctly label these islands, water resources, and other important landforms. Spelling Counts!

ISLANDS
Antigua
Bahamas
Bay Islands
Cayman Islands
Cuba
Dominica
Grenada
Hispaniola
Jamaica
Margarita
Martinique
Puerto Rico
Saint Kitts
Saint Martin
Tobago
Trinidad
Virgin Islands

WATER RESOURCES
Caribbean Sea

OTHER LANDFORMS
Central America
Panama
South America

Name _____

CHRISTOPHER COLUMBUS

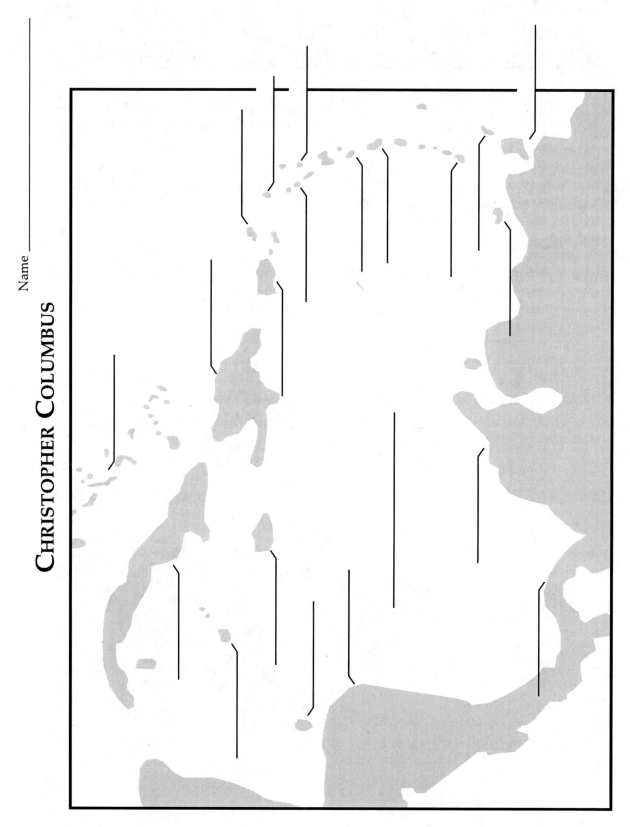

MAPPING: ISLANDS, WATER RESOURCES, AND LANDFORMS

You have just finished reading about Christopher Columbus's voyages to the New World. During his voyages, Columbus named many of the islands in the Caribbean Sea.

In this activity, you will label many of these islands, water **resources**, and other important landforms and on a blank map.

Directions:

Using the blank map on the next page and your information about Christopher Columbus, correctly label these islands, water resources, and other important landforms. Spelling Counts!

ISLANDS
Antigua
Bahamas
Bay Islands
Cayman Islands
Cuba
Dominica
Grenada
Hispaniola
Jamaica
Margarita
Martinique
Puerto Rico
Saint Kitts
Saint Martin
Tobago
Trinidad
Virgin Islands

WATER RESOURCES
Caribbean Sea

OTHER LANDFORMS
Central America
Panama
South America

CHRISTOPHER COLUMBUS

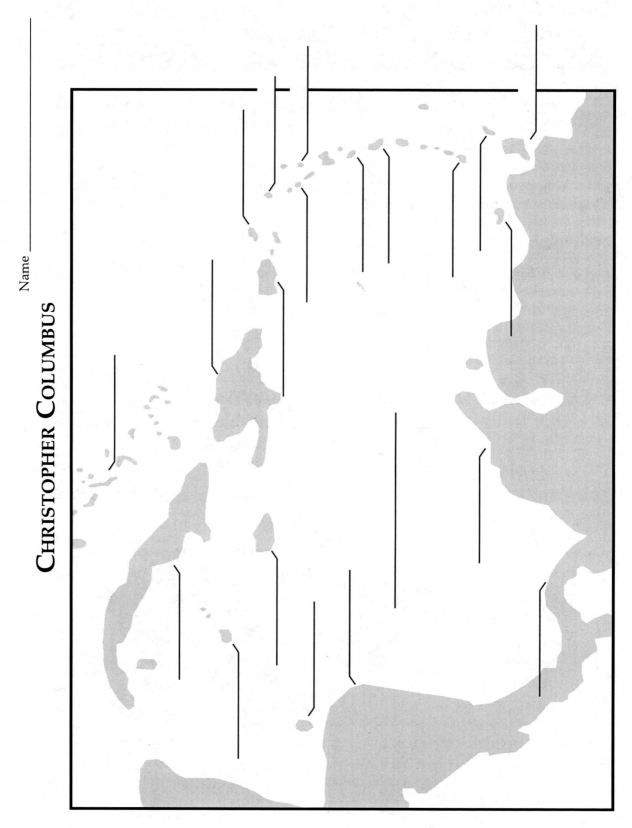

∼∼∼∼∼ VOCABULARY QUIZ ∼∼∼∼∼

SPANISH EXPLORERS AND CONQUISTADORS
PART I

Directions: Match the vocabulary word on the left with its definition on the right. Put the letter for the definition on the blank next to the vocabulary word it matches. Use each word and definition only once.

1. _____ witnesses

2. _____ appointed

3. _____ accused

4. _____ West Indies

5. _____ voyage

6. _____ coast

7. _____ Caribbean Sea

8. _____ conquered

9. _____ torture

10. _____ tavern

11. _____ stranded

12. _____ continent

13. _____ convinced

14. _____ Hispaniola

15. _____ historians

16. _____ strait

A. one of seven large areas of land on the globe.

B. a chain of islands in the Caribbean Sea that stretches from the southern tip of Florida to the northeastern corner of South America.

C. a buyer or seller whose goal is to make money.

D. one of seven continents in the world. Bounded by Alaska on the northwest, Greenland on the northeast, Florida on the southeast, and Mexico on the southwest.

E. people who are called upon to tell the truth about what they heard or saw.

F. a public place that sells alcoholic beverages.

G. the world's largest continent with more than half of the Earth's population.

H. an arm of the Atlantic Ocean surrounded on the north and east by the West Indies, on the south by South America, and on the west by Central America.

I. people who study history.

J. a large piece of land set apart from an island.

K. a person from Europe, the sixth smallest of Earth's seven continents.

L. very uncomfortable conditions.

M. blamed or charged with a crime.

N. a sheltered area where ships can load and unload supplies.

O. journey that is usually made by water.

17. _____ seaport

18. _____ estimated

19. _____ European

20. _____ geography

21. _____ resources

22. _____ Portugal

23. _____ native

24. _____ harsh

25. _____ governor

26. _____ ignored

27. _____ North America

28. _____ inhabitants

29. _____ New World

30. _____ navigation

31. _____ islands

32. _____ journal

33. _____ merchant

34. _____ mainland

35. _____ kidnapped

36. _____ Asia

P.   the study of the Earth's surface.

Q.   a narrow strip of sea between two pieces of land.

R.   areas of land that are completely surrounded by water.

S.   people who live or settle in a place.

T.   belonging to a place because you were born there.

U.   talked someone into doing something your way.

V.   things found in nature that are valuable to humans.

W.   chosen or selected.

X.   took someone without permission.

Y.   left alone without any help.

Z.   didn't listen to.

AA. guessed.

BB. a term once used to describe the continents of North America and South America.

CC. defeated by force.

DD. a written record of daily events.

EE. an area of land that borders water.

FF. controlling the direction of a ship.

GG. a country along the Atlantic Ocean on the southwestern edge of Europe whose capital is Lisbon.

HH. to cause severe physical or mental pain to someone.

II.   an island in the West Indies that lies between Cuba and Puerto Rico.

JJ.   a person who is in charge of an area or group.

AMERIGO VESPUCCI

Amerigo Vespucci (veh•SPOO•chee) was born on March 9, 1454, to a wealthy family in Florence, Italy. As a child, he was educated by his uncle who taught him math, science, and Latin. Amerigo's hobbies were collecting books and copying maps. He dreamed of traveling so he could see what the Earth really looked like.

As an adult, Amerigo became a businessman. He hoped to make enough money so he could explore. In 1491, Amerigo moved to Spain. He became the director of a company that supplied explorers with everything they needed for their long voyages. When Christopher Columbus returned from his first journey to the New World, it was probably Amerigo's company that supplied him with food and tools for his second and third voyages.

VESPUCCI'S VOYAGES TO THE NEW WORLD

Historians can't completely agree on how many voyages Amerigo Vespucci made to the New World. Some think he made his first voyage for Spain in 1497. Others believe he did not sail toward the New World until 1499. They do agree that during one or both of these **expeditions**, Spain sent Vespucci to find a shorter route to Asia. Finding a quick route to Asia would give Spain control of Asia's jewels, silk, and spices.

Vespucci sailed from Cadiz, Spain. He reached the mouth of the Amazon River and touched the mainland of Brazil in South America. Some believe he entered the Gulf of Mexico in the present-day United States. Using the position of the planets and the stars, Vespucci was able to figure out how far west he had traveled.

AMERIGO VESPUCCI

SAILING FOR PORTUGAL (POR•CHUW•GAL)

In the early 1500s, Vespucci made voyages that were paid for by Portugal. Each time, he sailed from the city of Lisbon and followed the South American coast. During one of these expeditions, he sailed within 400 miles of the southern tip of South America.

Vespucci wrote letters to his friends in Europe describing his travels. He did not find a shorter route to Asia. He was, however, the first explorer to discover that North and South America were actually separate from Asia. Remember, Christopher Columbus thought he had sailed to Asia when his ships landed in the West Indies off the southeast coast of North America.

HONORING AMERIGO VESPUCCI

In 1508, Spain named Amerigo Vespucci as Pilot Major. This was a very high honor. It meant that Vespucci was the most skilled navigator in the entire world. He would not live long enough to enjoy this honor. Four years later, Amerigo Vespucci died of **malaria**.

A year before Vespucci's death, German **scholar** Martin Waldseemuller read about Vespucci's discoveries. In honor of Amerigo Vespucci, Waldseemuller printed a wood block map with the name "America" spread across the southern continent of the New World. More than 1,000 copies of Waldseemuller's map were sold throughout Europe.

A few years later, Waldseemuller changed his mind about the name America. It was too late. The word America had stuck. In 1538, a map of the world was created. It honored Amerigo Vespucci by naming the northern and southern continents of the New World, North America and South America.

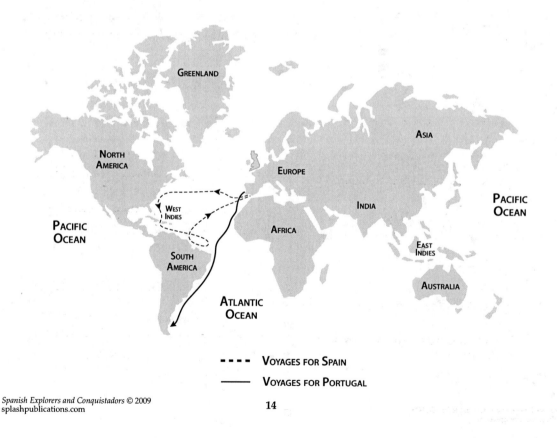

AMERIGO VESPUCCI

Directions: Read each question carefully. Darken the circle for the correct answer.

1 **What were Amerigo Vespucci's hobbies as a child?**

A Collecting stamps and baseball cards.

B Playing baseball and soccer.

C Playing outside with his friends.

D Copying maps and collecting books.

2 **About how many voyages did Vespucci make to the New World?**

F Less than three.

G Historians can't agree on how many voyages he made.

H At least ten.

J He never made it to the New World.

3 **Amerigo Vespucci was the first explorer to discover that –**

A the West Indies were full of Native Americans

B Christopher Columbus had actually found Asia

C North and South America are separate from Asia

D it is impossible to tell how far you have sailed in a ship

4 **In 1508, Spain named Amerigo Vespucci as Pilot Major. What did this honor mean?**

F He was in charge of Spain's army and navy.

G He was given money to build airplanes so he could fly around the world.

H He could make a map with his name on it.

J He was the most skilled navigator in the world.

5 **After reading about Martin Waldseemuller's map, you get the idea that –**

A it's difficult to change peoples' minds about something

B he made the map after Vespucci died

C Waldseemuller wasn't a very smart man

D the map was given away to a few of Waldseemuller's friends and family

6 **What can you learn by studying the map of Amerigo Vespucci's voyages?**

F Both voyages were paid for by Spain.

G Both voyages were paid for by Portugal.

H He visited the West Indies while sailing for Portugal.

J His voyages for Portugal took him farther south than his voyages for Spain.

7 **Which statement about Amerigo Vespucci's voyages is <u>true</u>?**

A He was the first explorer to reach Asia.

B He sailed around the world.

C His voyages took him to the coasts of North and South America.

D Like other explorers, he sailed around the tip of Africa.

READING

Answers

1 Ⓐ Ⓑ Ⓒ Ⓓ   5 Ⓐ Ⓑ Ⓒ Ⓓ

2 Ⓕ Ⓖ Ⓗ Ⓙ   6 Ⓕ Ⓖ Ⓗ Ⓙ

3 Ⓐ Ⓑ Ⓒ Ⓓ   7 Ⓐ Ⓑ Ⓒ Ⓓ

4 Ⓕ Ⓖ Ⓗ Ⓙ

consider
the source

Think about the resources we use to learn about history. Reading books, seeing movies, looking at photographs, studying maps, searching the Internet, digging for bones, and holding pieces of pottery are some of the ways that we learn about the past.

There are two types of sources to help us learn about what happened in the past. Primary sources are recorded by people who were there at the time. If you have ever read a diary or an **autobiography**, then you were reading something that was written by the person who was actually recording the events and experiences as they were happening. Diaries and autobiographies are primary sources. Letters, interviews, photographs, original maps, bones, and pieces of pottery are other examples of primary sources because they give us "first-hand" knowledge of an event that took place in history.

Secondary sources are recorded by people after an event took place. Many books have been written about important historical events and people. A book written in 1963 about the life of Christopher Columbus is a secondary source because the author wasn't actually there to interview the famous explorer and can't give any "first-hand" knowledge. Movies, **biographies,** newspaper stories, and encyclopedias are other examples of secondary sources because they give us "second-hand" knowledge of events that took place in history.

You have just finished studying about Spanish explorers Christopher Columbus and Amerigo Vespucci.

In this activity, you will decide whether a source of information is a primary source or a secondary source. On the lines provided, put a "P" next to the primary sources and an "S" next to the secondary sources.

1. _____ A piece of wood from one of Christopher Columbus's ships **preserved** in a museum.

2. _____ One of Martin Waldseemuller's wood block maps with the name America on it.

3. _____ A page from Christopher Columbus's journal.

4. _____ Amerigo Vespucci's biography.

5. _____ A picture of the *Niña*, the *Pinta*, and the *Santa Maria* drawn by your brother.

6. _____ The original letters that Amerigo Vespucci wrote to his friends in Europe.

7. _____ The map that Christopher Columbus drew with the names of the islands in the Caribbean Sea.

VASCO NÚÑEZ DE BALBOA

Vasco Núñez de Balboa was born in Spain. It's not clear exactly when he was born, but most historians agree that it was probably in 1475. His parents were not wealthy, so young Vasco worked in the household of a rich **nobleman** who lived on the Atlantic Coast of southwest Spain. Many ships heading for the New World stopped here to pick of supplies and crew members. As sailors returned from their voyages, Vasco heard the stories of land and riches across the Atlantic Ocean.

VOYAGE TO SOUTH AMERICA

In 1501, Balboa joined a Spanish expedition to South America. The expedition explored the northern coast of present-day Colombia. The group was not able to settle in Colombia because they didn't have enough men, food, or supplies. Instead, they sailed through the Caribbean Sea to the island of Hispaniola (his•pan•ee•OH•luh).

Balboa used the money he earned from the South American expedition to purchase land and pigs. Unfortunately, the Native Americans on the island of Hispaniola **worshipped** pigs. They would not buy or eat animals that they worshipped.

Unable to successfully farm or raise pigs, Balboa soon found himself poor and in **debt**. He wanted to leave Hispaniola and join an expedition that was planning to build the **colony** of San Sebastián in South America. The people to whom he owed money would not allow him to leave.

In 1510, Balboa left Hispaniola by hiding on a ship that was taking supplies to San Sebastián. The captain discovered Balboa hiding in a barrel. He threatened to throw him off the ship. Balboa's life was saved because he convinced the captain that his knowledge of the area they were going to could be useful. When they reached San Sebastián, they found that the colonists had **abandoned** the settlement because of Native American attacks.

Santa María

Balboa suggested that they move the colony west to Darién (DAIR•ree•an). According to Balboa, **fertile** soil and friendlier Native Americans could be found in this area of South America. When they arrived at the spot that Balboa had told them about, they found 500 **hostile** Native American warriors ready to fight. After a difficult battle, the Spaniards successfully **defeated** the Native Americans. They **raided** the Native American village and discovered a treasure of golden ornaments. They named their new settlement Santa María. Santa María was the first permanent settlement on the mainland of South America.

Governor Balboa

As a reward for his leadership, Vasco Balboa was chosen as the governor of Santa María. As governor, Balboa had complete power. From his settlement in Santa María, Governor Balboa sailed west along Panama's coastline, defeating some Native Americans and making friends with others. He explored rivers, mountains, and swamps, searching for gold and capturing slaves. He claimed huge areas of new land for Spain. Balboa wrote to the king of Spain asking for more men, weapons, and supplies for building ships.

Balboa planted corn and received fresh supplies from Hispaniola and Spain. He got his men ready for exploring. He collected a large amount of gold from the ornaments worn by the Native American women. Some of this gold was given to him; most of it he took by force.

In 1513, Governor Balboa heard stories about an area to the south where people were so rich that they ate and drank from dishes made of solid gold. Balboa was warned that he would need at least 1,000 men to defeat the Native Americans living along the coast of what they called "the other sea."

DISCOVERING THE SOUTH SEA

On September 1, 1513, Balboa led an expedition of about 200 Spaniards, a few Native American guides and a pack of dogs across the **Isthmus of Panama**. The group included famous explorer Francisco Pizarro (puh•ZAR•roh), whom you will learn about soon. Using a small ship and ten Native American canoes, the group sailed along the coast until they met up with a tribe of Native Americans that Balboa had **befriended**. They left the Native American village with more than 1,000 men ready for battle. Balboa led his army through 45 miles of Panama's jungle.

Thirty days later, the expedition reached the sea that Balboa had been told about. Balboa walked into the ocean, dipped his sword in the water, and claimed the water and all of the surrounding land for Spain. He named the new sea Mar del Sur, which means South Sea in English. Today, we know this body of water as the Pacific Ocean.

The most important reason for Balboa's journey was to find the gold. His large army of Spaniards and Native American warriors easily defeated the native peoples living along the South Sea. As promised, Balboa found riches of gold and pearls. He then learned that more treasure could be found on a group of islands guarded by a powerful and feared tribe of Native Americans. Balboa and a small group of warriors paddled canoes to reach the islands. After a bloody battle, Balboa and his army defeated the Native Americans on the islands. They took as much gold and pearls as they could carry in their canoes. Before leaving, Balboa named the largest island Isla Rica, which means Rich Island.

PEDRO ARIAS

On January 19, 1514, Balboa returned to Santa María a very wealthy man. More importantly, he had discovered the South Sea and claimed new land for Spain. As required by Spanish law, Balboa sent one fifth of his treasure to King Ferdinand in Spain.

Since Balboa had been gone for so long, King Ferdinand chose a new governor for Santa María. His name was Pedro Arias. In July 1514, Pedro Arias arrived in Santa María with men, women, and supplies.

Balboa was angry that he had been replaced as governor. He wanted more than anything to return to the South Sea and continue searching for pearls and gold. Unfortunately, Balboa was no longer in power. It was the governor's job to decide which explorers led expeditions.

Balboa secretly planned his next expedition. Governor Arias found out about Balboa's plans and had him arrested. Just as Governor Arias was planning to lock Balboa in a wooden cage, King Ferdinand received news of Balboa's discoveries and one fifth of the treasure that Balboa had sent. The king saved Balboa's life.

King Ferdinand told Governor Arias that Balboa was to be shown the greatest **respect** for all of his accomplishments. Governor Arias obeyed the king. He even arranged for Balboa to marry one of his daughters.

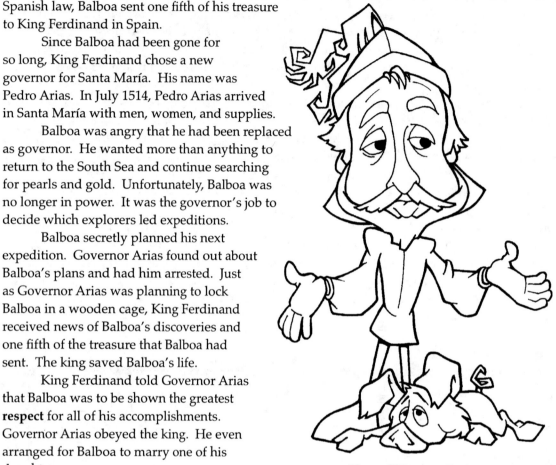

VASCO NÚÑEZ DE BALBOA

BALBOA'S DEATH

In 1517, Governor Arias permitted Balboa to return to the South Sea. On his way back to Santa María, Balboa was arrested by Francisco Pizarro, the same soldier who had been with him when he discovered the South Sea. Pizarro had been sent by Governor Arias. Balboa was accused of trying to take control of the South Sea for himself. Balboa **denied** all charges and demanded to be taken to Spain where he could speak with King Ferdinand and receive a fair trial. Governor Arias refused. He ordered that the trial take place immediately.

On January 15, 1519, Vasco Balboa and four of his friends were found guilty of **treason**. They were sentenced to death. As Balboa was led to the chopping block to have his head removed, he screamed, "Lies, lies! Never have such crimes held a place in my heart. I have always **loyally** served the King, with no thought in my mind but to increase his **dominions**." After Balboa and his four friends were **beheaded**, their heads were put on public display for several days.

~~~~~~~~ VASCO NÚÑEZ DE BALBOA ~~~~~~~~

Directions: Read each question carefully. Darken the circle for the correct answer.

1   **After reading the first paragraph about Vasco Nuñez de Balboa, you get the idea that –**

   A   his parents gave him everything he wanted

   B   historians know exactly when he was born

   C   he listened to sailors tell their stories

   D   he was born in Italy

2   **What did Balboa do with the money he earned from the expedition to South America?**

   F   He purchased land and pigs.

   G   He sent it to his parents in Spain.

   H   He paid for another trip to South America.

   J   He returned to Spain and became a farmer.

3   **Which phrase about Balboa tells you that he was able to talk his way out of difficult situations?**

   A   ...Balboa soon found himself poor and in debt...

   B   ...hiding on a ship that was taking supplies to San Sebastián...

   C   ...captain discovered Balboa hiding in a barrel...

   D   ...convinced the captain that he was valuable...

4   **Which statement about Governor Balboa is <u>false</u>?**

   F   He claimed land for Spain.

   G   He took whatever he wanted.

   H   He didn't have any power in Santa María.

   J   As governor, he searched for gold and captured slaves.

5   **Which body of water did Balboa discover?**

   A   Pacific Ocean

   B   Atlantic Ocean

   C   Gulf of Mexico

   D   Caribbean Sea

6   **What was more important to Balboa than discovering this body of water?**

   F   Rescuing the Native Americans from Isla Rica.

   G   Making sure his soldiers were safe and well rested.

   H   Finding the gold that others had told him about.

   J   Returning safely to Santa María.

7   **What was Balboa's punishment for being found guilty of treason?**

   A   He was sent back to Spain.

   B   He was beheaded.

   C   He spent the rest of his life in a wooden cage.

   D   He was hanged.

8   **If Balboa had been permitted to return to Spain for a trial, he <u>probably</u> -**

   F   would have been found not guilty

   G   would have been put to death anyway

   H   would still be alive today

   J   would have told King Ferdinand about how fairly he was treated by Governor Arias

READING

Answers

1 Ⓐ Ⓑ Ⓒ Ⓓ   5 Ⓐ Ⓑ Ⓒ Ⓓ
2 Ⓕ Ⓖ Ⓗ Ⓙ   6 Ⓕ Ⓖ Ⓗ Ⓙ
3 Ⓐ Ⓑ Ⓒ Ⓓ   7 Ⓐ Ⓑ Ⓒ Ⓓ
4 Ⓕ Ⓖ Ⓗ Ⓙ   8 Ⓕ Ⓖ Ⓗ Ⓙ

Grid Math is a fun way to learn an important skill. Grids are used to find places on maps, to track weather patterns, and in space exploration.

For Example: If you want to locate a place where C meets 3 (C,3), you would go **over** to C and **up** to 3. On a map or an atlas, (C,3) may be the place where you would find the name of your city.

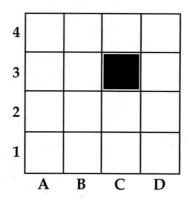

Directions: In this activity you will use a grid system to put together a puzzle that should remind you of Spanish **conquistador** (con•KEE•stah•dor) Vasco Nuñez de Balboa. You will need the 48 puzzle pieces (some of the puzzle pieces are below and the rest of them are on the next page), and the blank grid.

1. Cut out the puzzle pieces **one at a time** (cut around the thick black line of the square). Glue **that** piece in its proper place on the empty grid before cutting out the next piece. Make sure that you do not turn the puzzle piece upside down or turn it on its side before gluing it; the way it looks before you cut it out is the way it should be glued onto the grid.

2. Follow the example above: If the puzzle piece is labeled **(D,1)**, glue that piece in the space where D meets 1 on the grid by going <u>over</u> to D and <u>up</u> to 1. **(D,1)** has been done for you as an example.

3. When you are finished, color in your picture with your coloring pencils.

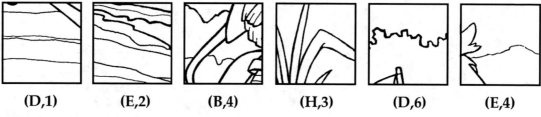

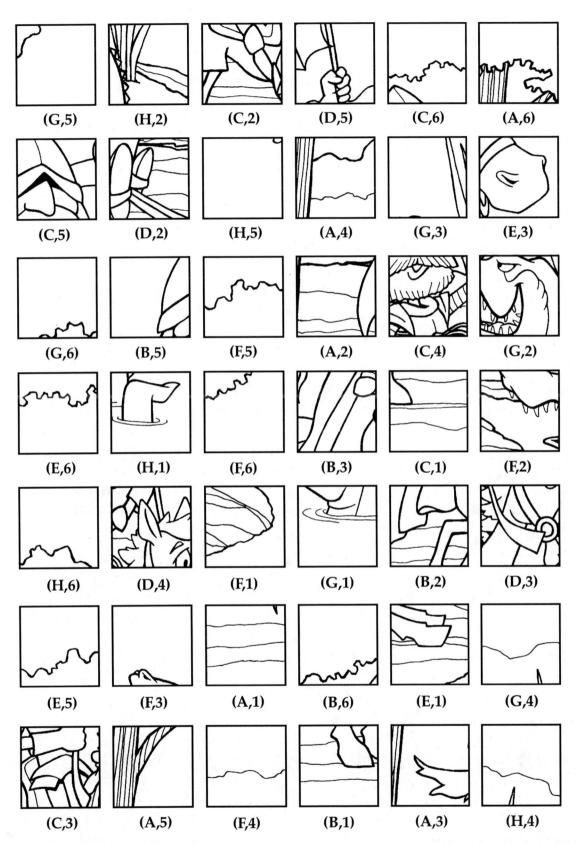

(G,5)   (H,2)   (C,2)   (D,5)   (C,6)   (A,6)

(C,5)   (D,2)   (H,5)   (A,4)   (G,3)   (E,3)

(G,6)   (B,5)   (F,5)   (A,2)   (C,4)   (G,2)

(E,6)   (H,1)   (F,6)   (B,3)   (C,1)   (F,2)

(H,6)   (D,4)   (F,1)   (G,1)   (B,2)   (D,3)

(E,5)   (F,3)   (A,1)   (B,6)   (E,1)   (G,4)

(C,3)   (A,5)   (F,4)   (B,1)   (A,3)   (H,4)

NAME _____

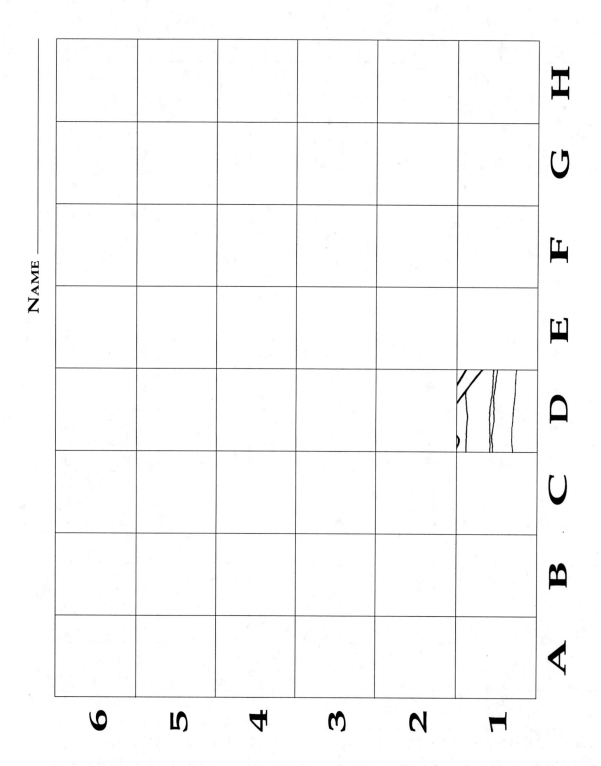

A   B   C   D   E   F   G   H

6
5
4
3
2
1

JUAN PONCE DE LEÓN

Juan Ponce (PON•say) de León was born in Spain. Historians believe that he was probably born in 1460. As a child growing up in a poor family, Juan earned money delivering messages and packages. During the early 1490s, he served in the Spanish Army and fought to drive the **Muslims** out of Spain.

VOYAGE TO THE NEW WORLD

In 1493, Juan Ponce de León sailed with Christopher Columbus during the famous explorer's second voyage to the New World. He did not return to Spain with Columbus. He stayed in Hispaniola (his•pan•ee•OH•luh) and led the defeat of the island's Native Americans. For his bravery, the Spanish government appointed Ponce de León as governor of a **province** on the island. He was also given permission to explore Puerto Rico, where he had heard gold could be found.

GOVERNOR OF PUERTO RICO

In 1509, Ponce de León claimed Puerto Rico for Spain and **founded** the island's first settlement. Once again, the Spanish government rewarded Ponce de León by appointing him as governor of Puerto Rico. The Native Americans in Puerto Rico were treated very badly by Governor Ponce de León. They were forced to dig for gold that would make Governor Ponce de León rich. He also made the Native Americans build forts to protect Spain's claim on Puerto Rico. While Ponce de León became a wealthy man, many of the Native Americans died from his poor treatment and diseases brought by the island's new European settlers.

JUAN PONCE DE LEÓN

In 1512, the Spanish government gave Ponce de León permission to explore the lands north of Cuba. Any land that Ponce de León discovered would be under his control for life. According to **legend**, Caribbean natives told Ponce de León about springs on the island of Bimini in the Bahamas that gave all who drank from them **eternal** life and health. Ponce de León was interested in finding this "Fountain of Youth."

DISCOVERING FLORIDA

In 1513, Juan Ponce de León sailed from Puerto Rico with three ships and about 200 men. Instead of finding the island of Bimini, they reached the east coast of present-day Florida in St. Augustine. Ponce de León claimed all of Florida for Spain and named the area "Pascua de Florida" which means "land of flowers."

Ponce de León and his crew left Florida and sailed toward Cuba. Again he tried unsuccessfully to find the island of Bimini and the mysterious "Fountain of Youth." He returned to Puerto Rico and then sailed back to Spain. In 1514, he was named Captain General by King Ferdinand II.

Juan Ponce de León made other voyages to the New World to search for gold and the "Fountain of Youth." In 1521, he sailed back to Florida where he planned to start a colony. The new settlement was under constant attack by Native Americans. Fighting broke out and Ponce de León was wounded by a Native American arrow. He returned to Cuba, where he died from his injury. Juan Ponce de León was buried in San Juan, Puerto Rico.

Name _____

Directions: Read each question carefully. Darken the circle for the correct answer.

1   After reading the first two paragraphs about Juan Ponce de León, you get the idea that he –

A   enjoyed fighting and conquering people

B   followed Christopher Columbus everywhere he went

C   grew up in a wealthy family

D   was never rewarded for his bravery

2   What can you conclude about Governor Ponce de León's treatment of Puerto Rico's Native Americans?

F   He treated them like family.

G   He gave them whatever they wanted.

H   He paid them for the work they did in Puerto Rico.

J   His poor treatment of Puerto Rico's Native Americans led to many of their deaths.

3   In the Bahamas, Ponce de León was searching for –

A   gold

B   the Fountain of Youth

C   Native American slaves

D   Christopher Columbus's son, Diego

4   Instead of reaching the Bahamas, where did Ponce de León land?

F   Puerto Rico

G   Jamaica

H   Asia

J   Florida

5   What does the phrase "Pascua de Florida" mean in English?

A   Fountain of Youth

B   Native American Land

C   Land of Flowers

D   Land of Love

6   What happened to Ponce de León's colony in Florida?

F   It was constantly attacked by Native Americans.

G   It was the most successful settlement in the history of Spain.

H   It was moved to Texas.

J   It grew too large and had to be divided into two colonies.

7   What can you learn from studying the map of Ponce de León's voyages?

A   Puerto Rico is west of Jamaica.

B   The Bahamas are north of Cuba.

C   The Gulf of Mexico is east of Florida.

D   Hispaniola is north of Florida.

8   According to the map, Cuba is –

F   southeast of Jamaica

G   southwest of Hispaniola

H   northwest of Florida

J   southwest of the Bahamas

READING

Answers

1 Ⓐ Ⓑ Ⓒ Ⓓ   5 Ⓐ Ⓑ Ⓒ Ⓓ
2 Ⓕ Ⓖ Ⓗ Ⓙ   6 Ⓕ Ⓖ Ⓗ Ⓙ
3 Ⓐ Ⓑ Ⓒ Ⓓ   7 Ⓐ Ⓑ Ⓒ Ⓓ
4 Ⓕ Ⓖ Ⓗ Ⓙ   8 Ⓕ Ⓖ Ⓗ Ⓙ

~~~~~ VOCABULARY QUIZ ~~~~~
SPANISH EXPLORERS AND CONQUISTADORS
PART II

Directions: Match the vocabulary word on the left with its definition on the right. Put the letter for the definition on the blank next to the vocabulary word it matches. Use each word and definition only once.

1. _____ province

2. _____ worshipped

3. _____ scholar

4. _____ malaria

5. _____ denied

6. _____ treason

7. _____ Muslims

8. _____ legend

9. _____ respect

10. _____ expeditions

11. _____ autobiography

12. _____ raided

13. _____ founded

14. _____ nobleman

A. people who follow the laws of Islam and worship God whom they call Allah.

B. started or established.

C. a settlement of people who are ruled by another country.

D. honored someone; usually during a religious ceremony.

E. angry and unfriendly.

F. the story of your life written by you.

G. a Spanish soldier who conquered the Native Americans of Mexico and Peru.

H. on the outside.

I. didn't agree to.

J. won victory over.

K. faithfully.

L. large territories with one ruler.

M. a well educated person who is a specialist on a subject.

15. _____ biographies

16. _____ loyally

17. _____ external

18. _____ abandoned

19. _____ Isthmus of Panama

20. _____ befriended

21. _____ hostile

22. _____ beheaded

23. _____ fertile

24. _____ colony

25. _____ dominions

26. _____ conquistador

27. _____ debt

28. _____ defeated

29. _____ preserved

N. a disease caused by mosquitoes that spreads to other humans and results in chills and fever.

O. the narrow strip of land connecting North and South America.

P. protected from injury or ruin so more can be learned.

Q. rich soil that produces a large number of crops.

R. a crime against your country's government.

S. stories of a person's life written by someone else.

T. journeys for the purpose of exploring.

U. a story told over and over again throughout history that can't be proven to be true.

V. money that is owed to someone else.

W. entered someone's property for the purpose of stealing.

X. cut off someone's head.

Y. gave up completely.

Z. a part of a country having a government of its own.

AA. made friends with someone.

BB. to honor someone.

CC. a man born to high rank.

FERDINAND MAGELLAN

Ferdinand Magellan was born in the spring of 1480, in northern Portugal (POR•chuw•gal). At the age of 10, both of Ferdinand's parents died. To continue young Ferdinand's education, he was appointed as the queen's messenger in the royal court. It was here that he learned about many famous explorers and important information about navigating ships.

MAGELLAN'S FIRST VOYAGE

In 1505, Ferdinand Magellan sailed to India on a **military** expedition. He knew immediately that he wanted to navigate the sea.

Magellan had heard about Christopher Columbus's voyages. He wanted more than anything to become the famous explorer who finally found a shorter route to Asia with all of its spices, silk, and jewels.

King Manuel I of Portugal refused to give Magellan ships or supplies for a voyage to the **Spice Islands** in Asia. The Portuguese still felt the best route to Asia was around the tip of Africa. Unhappy with the king's decision, Magellan left his home in Portugal and moved to Spain. He married a Spanish woman and became a Spanish **citizen**.

Magellan presented his plan to the king of Spain. He told King Charles V that

FERDINAND MAGELLAN

he knew of a secret strait through the southern continent of the New World. He believed he could sail right through this strait to the Spice Islands. If he could not find the strait, Magellan promised that he would sail back and follow the usual route around the tip of Africa. Either way, Magellan promised King Charles V that he would bring back spices and valuable treasure for Spain.

SAILING FOR SPAIN

King Charles V supported Magellan's plan. He gave Magellan permission to search for a shorter route to Asia. On August 15, 1519, Magellan set sail with five ships and more than 260 men. They took items to trade with the Native Americans and enough food to last for two years. Magellan kept his plans very secret. He didn't even tell the captains of his five ships where they were going.

THE STRAIT OF MAGELLAN

On December 15, 1519, Magellan's ships landed on the coast of present-day Brazil. They met friendly Native Americans who traded with them for fruit and fresh meat. They continued sailing south, looking for the secret strait that would take them to Asia. They found several **bays** and rivers, but no straits.

After another ten months of sailing, Magellan's ships found the strait they had been searching for. It took almost a month for his ships to sail through the 373 mile long passage that Magellan named All Saints **Channel**. He chose this name because his ships sailed through the passage on November 1, or All Saints Day. Today we call the passage the Strait of Magellan.

On November 28, 1520, Magellan's ships made it through the Strait of Magellan and sailed into a body of water Magellan had never seen before. He had no idea, of course, that this was the South Sea discovered by Spanish conquistador (con•KEE•stah•dor) Vasco Núñez de Balboa. Balboa had discovered and named the South Sea in 1513.

Magellan started sailing on his newly discovered ocean. He named it the Pacific because he found the water to be very peaceful. For the next three months, Magellan's ships sailed without finding any land. Without fresh drinking water or food, his crew was forced to eat rats. Many members of his crew died. Others suffered from **scurvy**.

FERDINAND MAGELLAN'S DEATH

On March 16, 1521, Magellan landed in the **Philippines**. He found many friendly natives on the islands that he visited. On the morning of April 17, 1521, Magellan sailed to the island of Mactan with 60 of his men. They were attacked by a tribe of 1,500 natives. Magellan was stabbed several times and died during the battle.

Magellan's men sailed on to the Spice Islands in the East Indies. They bought as many spices as they could hold in their two remaining ships. They also collected gold, pearls the size of hens' eggs, **porcelain**, eyeglasses, cinnamon, and **cloves**. As they left the Spice Islands, one of their ships began to sink and had to be left behind.

VOYAGE AROUND THE WORLD

On September 6, 1522, only one of Magellan's original five ships and less than 20 men made it safely back to Spain. The voyage took almost three years. Although he had only planned to sail to the Spice Islands in Asia, Ferdinand Magellan's expedition was the first to sail completely around the world. It was also the first to navigate the present-day Strait of Magellan connecting the Atlantic and Pacific oceans.

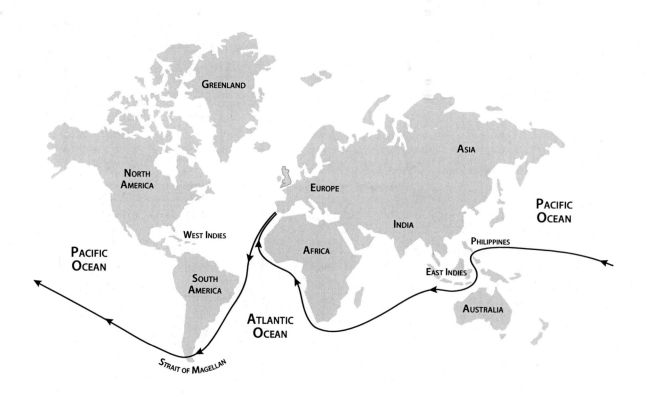

～～～～ FERDINAND MAGELLAN ～～～～

Directions: Read each question carefully. Darken the circle for the correct answer.

1 **Why did Portugal refuse to pay for Magellan's voyage to Asia?**

   A King Manuel I didn't like Magellan.

   B The Portuguese believed that the best route to Asia had already been discovered.

   C Portugal wasn't interested in Asian items like silk, spices, and jewels.

   D King Manuel I only supported voyages by citizens of Portugal and Magellan had been born in Spain.

2 **How did Magellan convince King Charles V of Spain to pay for his voyage to find a shorter route to Asia?**

   F Magellan promised that he would bring back valuable Asian spices and treasures even if he didn't find a shorter route to Asia.

   G Magellan agreed to marry the king's daughter.

   H Magellan promised to give the king half of everything he found.

   J Magellan agreed to take the king's son along on the voyage.

3 **The Strait of Magellan is a channel through South America. A channel is –**

   A a piece of land

   B a body of water

   C a large piece of land set apart from an island

   D a sheltered area where ships can load and unload supplies

4 **What can you learn by studying the map of the Strait of Magellan?**

   F The Strait of Magellan is north of the West Indies.

   G The Strait of Magellan cuts through South America.

   H The Strait of Magellan leads to the Gulf of Mexico.

   J The Strait of Magellan cuts through North America.

5 **Why did Magellan rename the South Sea the Pacific Ocean?**

   A It was the biggest ocean he had ever seen.

   B The waters of the ocean were very rough.

   C The Pacific Ocean was located in the north, not the south.

   D He found the water of the ocean to be very peaceful.

6 **Besides finding the Strait of Magellan, what else is Ferdinand Magellan famous for?**

   F Sailing around the world.

   G Discovering a shorter route to Asia.

   H Discovering and naming California.

   J Sailing safely around the tip of Africa.

READING

Answers

1 Ⓐ Ⓑ Ⓒ Ⓓ   4 Ⓕ Ⓖ Ⓗ Ⓙ
2 Ⓕ Ⓖ Ⓗ Ⓙ   5 Ⓐ Ⓑ Ⓒ Ⓓ
3 Ⓐ Ⓑ Ⓒ Ⓓ   6 Ⓕ Ⓖ Ⓗ Ⓙ

MAKE A MINIATURE GLOBE

In 1522, Ferdinand Magellan's expedition became the first to sail completely around the world.

In this activity, you will follow written directions to make a miniature globe that traces the famous route of the first voyage around the world.

1. Study the example below so that you can correctly color the Globe pattern.

   • The gray areas on the example are continents. Choose a color and shade in all of the continents.
   • The white areas on the example are oceans. Color the oceans and all of the round dots sticking out of the Globe blue.
   • Don't forget to color Magellan's ship!

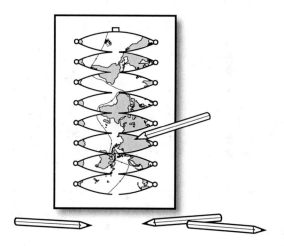

2. Cut out the Globe pattern along the bold black lines.

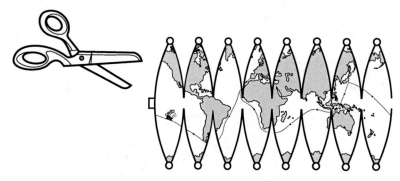

3. Glue Tab A to the opposite side of the Globe. (Make sure you tuck Tab A under so you can't see it after it's glued.)

4. Starting on the top of the Globe, glue the circles on top of one another. Turn the Globe over and glue all of those circles on top of one another.

5. Set the Globe aside so the glue can dry.

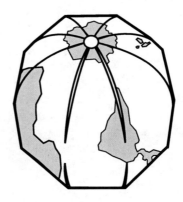

6. Color the Globe Stand pattern.

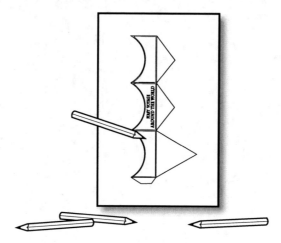

7. Cut out the Globe Stand pattern along the bold black lines.

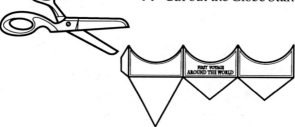

8. Fold the Globe Stand inward along the solid black lines. Fold Tab B down. Fold down each of the three triangles on the bottom of the Globe Stand.

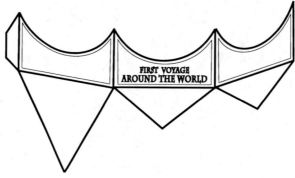

9. Fold the Globe Stand so that the largest triangle covers the entire bottom of the Stand. Glue Tab B under so you can't see it after it's glued.

10. Glue down the large triangle on the bottom of the Globe Stand.

11. Place the Globe in the Globe Stand. (Make sure Magellan's ship is right side up!)

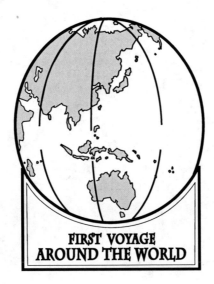

FIRST VOYAGE
AROUND THE WORLD

MAGELLAN GLOBE PATTERN

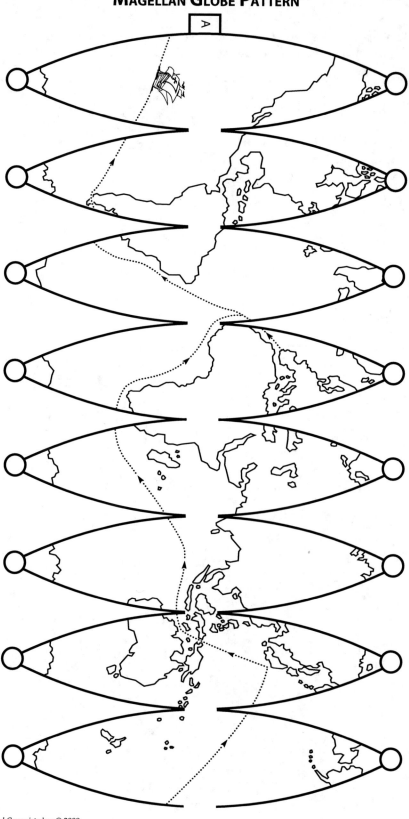

A

GLOBE STAND PATTERN

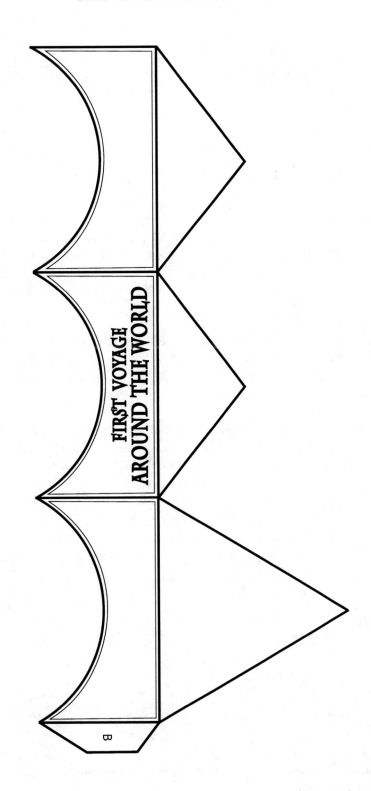

FIRST VOYAGE AROUND THE WORLD

B

HERNANDO CORTÉS

Hernando Cortés was born in Spain. Historians aren't sure the exact date of his birth, but most agree it was in 1485. He was the only boy in a family of four children. At the age of 14, Hernando's parents sent him to school at one of Spain's best universities. They hoped he would study Latin and become a lawyer. After only two years, Hernando returned home. Sixteen year old Hernando wasn't interested in studying anymore. He had heard about Christopher Columbus's discoveries. Hernando dreamed of sailing to the West Indies to search for gold and conquer new land.

CONQUERING CUBA

In 1503, eighteen year old Hernando Cortés arrived in Santo Domingo, the **capital** of Hispaniola (his•pan•ee•OH•luh). As a new citizen, he was given a piece of land for building a home and planting crops. In 1506, Cortés joined the Spanish military and helped take control of Cuba for Spain. For his bravery, he was rewarded with a large piece of land and many slaves.

In 1519, Hernando Cortés was sent from Cuba to the Gulf of Mexico. He was told to explore the area known as Mexico, trade with the natives found there, and bring slaves back to Cuba. He took horses, a few weapons, and 600 soldiers for his journey.

When his ship landed in Mexico, Hernando Cortés disobeyed the instructions of Cuba's leaders. He didn't plan to explore, trade, or take slaves back to Cuba. Instead, he claimed the land for Spain. He wanted to take control of Mexico and set up an **empire** for himself. The Aztec Empire stood in Hernando Cortés's way.

THE AZTEC EMPIRE

The Aztec people lived along the Gulf of Mexico. The Aztecs were fearless warriors who had created a huge empire that included many cities and towns. They built this empire by defeating other groups of people. The Aztecs would take control of their land and make them pay yearly taxes.

Warfare was considered a religious duty by the Aztecs. Prisoners taken during war were **sacrificed** to the gods.

The Aztecs designed their own calendar, built large temples for religious **ceremonies**, and created beautiful **sculptures**.

AZTEC FARMERS

The Aztecs were farmers who practiced slash-and-burn **agriculture**. They chopped down trees and burned a section of the forest, then planted crops in the clearing.

The ashes from the burned trees **fertilized** the soil. Aztec farmers also dug **canals** to **irrigate** their crops. They turned **shallow** lakes into farmland by scooping up mud from the lake bottoms to form islands. They planted seeds in the islands and regularly added mud to water the crops.

DEFEATING THE AZTECS

Hernando Cortés was able to easily **recruit** people who had been defeated by the Aztecs and were being forced to pay yearly taxes to them. It took three months for Cortés and his small army of volunteers to travel 300 miles to the capital of the Aztec Empire.

Hernando Cortés was greeted warmly by the Aztec **emperor**. He was given expensive gifts and even welcomed into the emperor's home. The emperor had no idea what Hernando Cortés had planned. Cortés immediately took the emperor prisoner and demanded that the Aztecs pay a **ransom** of gold and jewels for his safe return. The Aztecs began gathering treasures to pay the ransom. Cortés's plan fell apart after the emperor was accidentally struck in the head with a rock and died.

After the death of their emperor, the Aztecs attacked Cortés and his army. Cortés left the city for a short time but returned and formed a **blockade** around the entire city. The Aztecs were unable to get food or water. Thousands starved to death or died from disease. After the defeat, Hernando Cortés and his army destroyed the Aztec buildings and built Mexico City right on top of the ruins.

Governor Cortés

King Charles V appointed Hernando Cortés as governor of **New Spain**. Since the king didn't completely trust Hernando Cortés, four royal **officials** were also appointed to help Cortés. Governor Cortés founded more cities in New Spain. He appointed men to explore and conquer new land for Spain. Governor Cortés wanted Native Americans to give up their native **customs** and religious ceremonies and accept **Christianity**. Cortés was one of the first Spaniards to grow sugar cane in Spain. He was also the first to **import** black slaves from Africa into New Spain.

Governor Cortés was a very wealthy and powerful man. He used his power to lead an expedition to Honduras where he took control and had the governor arrested.

The leaders in Spain became very worried about how powerful Governor Cortés had become. Several men were sent from Spain to remove Governor Cortés from power. In 1528, Hernando Cortés was **exiled** from New Spain.

HERNANDO CORTÉS

Final Explorations and Death

Hernando Cortés returned to Spain. King Charles V rewarded him for **expanding** Spain's empire in New Spain. Cortés was given permission to return to New Spain and continue conquering new land. The king also gave Cortés land in one of the wealthiest areas of New Spain. He was not, however, permitted to return to power as governor of New Spain.

In 1530, Hernando Cortés returned to New Spain. He focused his time and energy on building his palace. In 1536, he explored the northwestern and Pacific coasts of Mexico and discovered present-day Baja or Lower California. He returned to Spain in 1541, and joined a military expedition to the **Barbary Coast**. During the voyage, he almost drowned in a storm.

After his last voyage, Hernando Cortés found himself deeply in debt. He had borrowed and spent most of his own money to pay for his expeditions. In 1547, Cortés planned to return to his palace in New Spain. He never made it back to his home. On December 2, 1547, Hernando Cortés died in Spain of **pleurisy** (PLEW•ruh•see).

~~~~~ HERNANDO CORTÉS ~~~~~

Directions: Read each question carefully. Darken the circle for the correct answer.

1 After reading the first paragraph about Hernando Cortés, you can conclude that –

  A his parents were disappointed in his choices

  B he was an only child

  C he wanted to go back to school, but his parents wouldn't let him

  D he wasn't really interested in sailing

2 In 1503, what was the capital of Hispaniola?

  F Santa María

  G Cuba

  H Mexico City

  J Santo Domingo

3 Which statement about Hernando Cortés is <u>true</u>?

  A He refused to join the Spanish military.

  B He had difficulty taking orders from others.

  C He was always interested in doing the right thing.

  D He cared about other people more than he cared about himself.

4 What can you learn from reading about the Aztec Empire?

  F They were shy and quiet.

  G They were warriors who sacrificed prisoners to the gods.

  H They didn't practice a religion of their own.

  J They survived by hunting and gathering roots and berries.

5 How did Hernando Cortés get into the Aztec emperor's home?

  A He crawled in through an open window.

  B He pretended that he was delivering flowers to the emperor.

  C He was invited in by the emperor.

  D He broke down the front door.

6 How did Aztec emperor die?

  F He was struck in the head with a rock.

  G He was shot with a bow and arrow.

  H He fell down a flight of stairs.

  J He became ill with malaria.

7 Which phrase tells you that the king of Spain didn't completely trust Hernando Cortés?

  A ...appointed Hernando Cortés as governor of New Spain...

  B ...used his power to lead an expedition to Honduras...

  C ...sent four royal officials to help Hernando Cortés...

  D ...gave him land in one of the wealthiest areas of New Spain...

READING

Answers

1 Ⓐ Ⓑ Ⓒ Ⓓ   5 Ⓐ Ⓑ Ⓒ Ⓓ
2 Ⓕ Ⓖ Ⓗ Ⓙ   6 Ⓕ Ⓖ Ⓗ Ⓙ
3 Ⓐ Ⓑ Ⓒ Ⓓ   7 Ⓐ Ⓑ Ⓒ Ⓓ
4 Ⓕ Ⓖ Ⓗ Ⓙ

Name _____

SPANISH CONQUISTADOR STORY

You have just finished reading about Hernando Cortés, one of the most famous Spanish conquistadors in history. Have you ever wondered what it would have been like to live back in the 1500s, and travel with Cortés to the Aztec Empire?

In this activity, you will travel back in time and write a story about your adventures as a Spanish conquistador.

Directions:
- Before beginning your story, organize your thoughts by answering the five questions on the next two pages.
- Write your rough draft on separate paper and have it edited. Make sure you include all of the details from the five questions you answered.
- Write your final draft on the special paper provided by your teacher. Attach extra paper if you need more space.
- Be prepared to read your story aloud to the rest of the class!

1. Give yourself a name and describe what you looked like. _____

_____

_____

_____

2. Describe two reasons for traveling to the New World.

   1. _____

      _____

      _____

   2. _____

      _____

      _____

3. Give details about two types of danger you faced during your journey to the New World.

    1. _____

       _____

       _____

    2. _____

       _____

       _____

4. Describe the job that Hernando Cortés gave you when you reached the Aztec Empire.

_____

_____

_____

_____

5. Describe how you felt after helping Hernando Cortés conquer the powerful Aztec Empire.

_____

_____

_____

_____

Now, use the details from these five questions to write your rough draft Spanish conquistador story. After your rough draft has been edited, write your final draft on the special paper provided by your teacher.

Name _____

ᔕᔕᔕᔕᔕ VOCABULARY QUIZ ᔕᔕᔕᔕᔕ
SPANISH EXPLORERS AND CONQUISTADORS
PART III

Directions: Match the vocabulary word on the left with its definition on the right. Put the letter for the definition on the blank next to the vocabulary word it matches. Use each word and definition only once.

1. _____ bays

2. _____ shallow

3. _____ channel

4. _____ sculptures

5. _____ citizen

6. _____ sacrificed

7. _____ cloves

8. _____ military

9. _____ recruit

10. _____ Philippines

11. _____ ransom

12. _____ pleurisy

13. _____ officials

14. _____ porcelain

A. the male ruler of an empire.

B. forced to leave.

C. growing larger.

D. a long, narrow, deep part of a body of water.

E. a hard white clay that is heated and glazed to make ceramic dishes.

F. waterways that bring water to crops.

G. to find people who are willing to join a military force.

H. a disease caused from lack of vitamin C that results in swollen and bleeding gums, bleeding under the skin, and extreme weakness.

I. shutting off a place to keep people and supplies from coming in or going out.

J. money paid for the safe return of a person who has been taken without permission.

K. bodies of water surrounded by land that open to the sea.

L. planting crops and raising farm animals.

M. figures or designs shaped out of clay, marble, or metal.

N. people with high rank who have the power to make decisions.

15. _____ irrigate

16. _____ import

17. _____ scurvy

18. _____ Spice Islands

19. _____ agriculture

20. _____ Barbary Coast

21. _____ blockade

22. _____ New Spain

23. _____ canals

24. _____ capital

25. _____ fertilized

26. _____ expanding

27. _____ ceremonies

28. _____ Christianity

29. _____ exiled

30. _____ empire

31. _____ customs

32. _____ emperor

O. a group of islands in Indonesia, a nation in southeast Asia.

P. added a material to the soil to make crops grow better.

Q. spices made from the dried flower buds of an evergreen tree.

R. pain in the lungs that causes chills, fever, and coughing.

S. religious or spiritual gatherings.

T. people who are part of the armed forces who may be asked to go to war.

U. Spanish colonies that were once in parts of North, Central, and South America.

V. a group of territories or peoples under one ruler.

W. a hole that is not very deep.

X. the city that serves as the center of government for the state or nation.

Y. killed an animal or human being as a spiritual offering.

Z. to water crops.

AA. a religion based on the life and teachings of Jesus Christ.

BB. person in a city, town, state, or country who enjoys the freedom to vote and participate in government decisions.

CC. the coast of the Mediterranean Sea where pirates went for protection.

DD. to bring items into a country for the purpose of selling them.

EE. usual ways of doing things.

FF. a group of islands southeast of China in the Pacific Ocean.

FRANCISCO PIZARRO

Francisco Pizarro (puh•ZAR•roh) was born in Spain. Some historians believe he may have been born in 1471. Others place his birthday in 1475 or 1478. They do agree that his father served in the Italian military and his second cousin was famous Spanish conquistador (con•KEE•stah•dor) Hernando Cortés.

VOYAGE TO THE NEW WORLD

On February 13, 1503, Francisco Pizarro made his first voyage to the New World. He sailed to Hispaniola (his•pan•ee•OH•luh) with 2,500 other colonists on a **fleet** of 30 ships. It was the largest fleet that had ever sailed to the New World.

In 1513, Pizarro joined Vasco Nuñez de Balboa's expedition to the South Sea. It was Francisco Pizarro who was sent to arrest Balboa when he had been accused of trying to take control of the South Sea for himself.

Balboa was found guilty of treason and beheaded for his crime. Pizarro was rewarded for his loyalty and appointed as the mayor of Panama City.

Several years later, Pizarro heard stories about a city filled with gold in present-day Peru. He knew about Hernando Cortés's defeat of the Aztec Empire.

FRANCISCO PIZARRO

Pizarro became interested in traveling to Peru. He wanted to conquer the people in Peru the way his cousin Hernando Cortés had conquered the Aztecs. To do this, he would have to defeat the Inca Empire.

THE INCA EMPIRE

The Inca ruled one of the largest and richest empires in the world. The empire stretched for more than 2,500 miles along the western coast of South America. They gained this huge territory by using their strong and powerful army of warriors to conquer Native American tribes in parts of Ecuador, Peru, Bolivia, Argentina, Chile, and Colombia. There were at least five million people living in the Inca Empire before the arrival of Spanish conquistadors.

The Inca Empire was connected by more than 10,000 miles of paved roads. Messages were carried by runners from one place to another in the huge empire. Most of the Inca cities were built on the steep slopes of the Andes Mountains. Stone steps led up to the top of the cities where stone houses and religious temples were built. The blocks of stones weighed several tons each. The stones fit together so tightly not even a piece of paper could pass between them. **Archaeologists** (ar•kee•OL•uh•jists) who have studied the Inca **culture** are still amazed that they were able to carry such heavy stones up so many steps.

There were different levels, or classes, in the Inca Empire. The emperor, high priest, and the army commander were at the top level. Family members of the emperor, including women related to the emperor, were on the next level. The temple priests, **architects**, and regional army commanders were on the third level. The two lowest classes were made up of **artisans**, soldiers, and farmers. Farmers were required to pay taxes in the form of gold to the higher classes. Inca wealth was displayed on the gold covered walls of the emperor's palace.

INCA FARMERS

The main crops of the Inca were corn, cotton, and potatoes. Inca farmers divided their fields into three groups. The **harvest** of one field went to the local people. The harvest of the other two fields supported the rulers and the empire's religious community. Like the Aztec culture you have read about, religion was very important to the Inca. No decision, no matter how small, was made without first praying to the gods. Human sacrifice was an important part of the Inca religion. Most people considered it an honor to be chosen for sacrifice.

CRIME AND PUNISHMENT

Punishment for crimes in the Inca Empire was very harsh. If someone lied, stole, or murdered, they were thrown off a cliff, had their hands cut off, their eyes cut out, or hung up to starve to death. There were no prisons built in the Inca Empire because most crimes were punished by death.

PIZARRO'S FIRST EXPEDITION

On September 13, 1524, Francisco Pizarro left from Panama with about 80 men and 40 horses. They sailed down the Pacific Coast, but reached no farther than Colombia. Bad weather, food shortages, and **conflicts** with Native Americans forced Pizarro to turn back to Panama.

PIZARRO'S SECOND EXPEDITION

Two years later, Pizarro was ready to try again. In August 1526, he left Panama with two ships and 160 men. Pizarro's ship made it as far as the San Juan River in Colombia. They stayed to explore the swampy area.

The other ship, navigated by Bartolomé Ruiz (roo•EZ), continued sailing south. After crossing the **equator**, Ruiz captured a group of natives from the Inca Empire who were carrying loads of **textiles**, ceramic objects, gold, silver, and jewels on rafts. Ruiz sailed back to the San Juan River with his **captives** to tell a tired and hungry Pizarro the good news. At the San Juan River, Pizarro and Ruiz were joined by Diego de Almagro (al•MAY•grow), 80 more men, and fresh supplies from Panama.

The group tried to sail back to the place where Ruiz had captured the Incas. Strong winds and dangerous ocean **currents** knocked them off course. They reached the coast of Ecuador where they found a very large group of Native Americans who were under Inca rule. Afraid for their safety, Pizarro and his group decided not to enter the land.

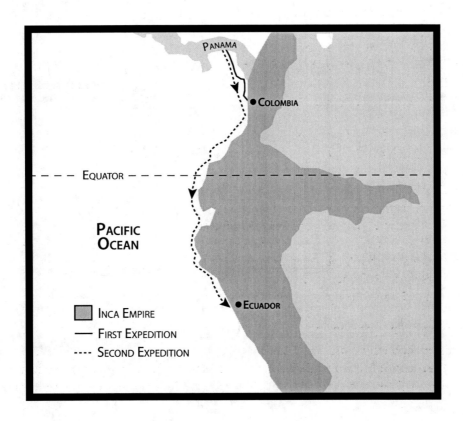

THE THIRTEEN OF THE FAME

Pizarro found a safe place near the coast on Gallo Island. He sent Diego de Almagro back to Panama for more men and supplies. The governor of Panama refused to send men or supplies to Pizarro. In fact, he ordered Pizarro to return to Panama immediately. Pizarro refused to return to Panama. Only 13 men decided to stay with him. They became known in history as the Thirteen of the Fame. The rest of his army, including Ruiz and Almagro, took the ships and returned to the safety of Panama.

Pizarro and his 13 men built a small boat and sailed nine miles north to Gorgona Island where they remained for seven months. They were once again joined by Diego de Almagro who had convinced the governor of Panama to give him a ship and supplies to rescue Pizarro and his 13 men. Almagro promised Panama's governor that as soon as Pizarro and his men were rescued, they would abandon the expedition. Of course, this was a lie.

REACHING THE INCA EMPIRE

In April 1528, Pizarro and his very small army reached the Tumbes (TOOM•bes) Region of the Inca Empire. The Incas warmly greeted Pizarro and his men. They were given food, water, and a place to stay. The natives had no idea what Pizarro and his men had planned.

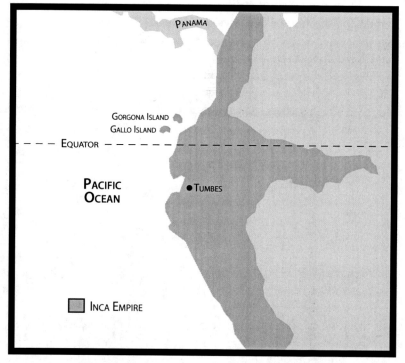

The Incas allowed Pizarro to freely explore their empire. He saw huge areas of land and more gold and silver than he could have ever imagined. He decided to return to Panama with this information so he could gather more men and supplies. He left two of his men so they could learn the customs and the language of the Incas.

Again, the governor of Panama refused to give Pizarro ships and men for another expedition to Peru. Pizarro sailed all the way to Spain and asked the king for permission. Francisco Pizarro's wish was granted. He was appointed governor of the new land he was about to conquer. The king gave Pizarro complete control of the next expedition to Peru.

PIZARRO'S THIRD EXPEDITION

On December 27, 1530, Pizarro left for his final voyage to Peru. He had three ships, 180 men, and 27 horses. Pizarro planned to **anchor** his ships in the Tumbes Region like he had done during his second expedition. Fearing that the Native Americans in Tumbes had been warned about Pizarro's plans, they landed instead on the island of Puná (POO•nuh). A battle broke out, leaving three of Pizarro's men and 400 Native Americans dead. After the battle, Pizarro's men raided the island, stealing as much gold, silver, and jewels as they could carry.

Pizarro and his men continued on land toward Peru. In July 1532, Pizarro established Peru's first Spanish settlement in a place he named San Miguel (mih•GEL).

Pizarro easily recruited Native Americans who had been conquered by the Incas. They spent the next two months walking south toward Cajamarca (cah•ha•MAR•cah), Peru. Pizarro planned to meet with the emperor. When they reached Cajamarca, the emperor refused to meet with Pizarro and his small army of less than 200 men. The emperor was not worried. He had 80,000 soldiers ready to defend the Inca Empire.

DEFEATING THE INCAS

On November 16, 1532, the Battle of Cajamarca was a surprise attack that lasted less than 30 minutes. The Incas were not prepared for Pizarro's army and their advanced weapons. During the attack, the emperor's 12 guards were killed and the Inca emperor was captured. Pizarro demanded a ransom of gold and silver for the emperor's safe return. Even after filling two rooms with silver and one room with gold, Pizarro had the emperor killed.

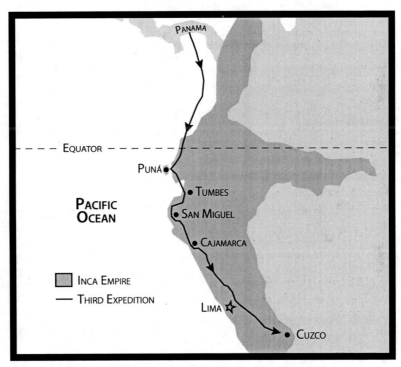

A year later, Pizarro and his forces **invaded** the Incan capital of Cuzco (COOZ•coh) in southeastern Peru. Taking control of Cuzco was the final step in completely defeating the Inca Empire. Pizarro claimed all of Peru for Spain and established the capital in the present-day city of Lima (LEE•muh). Pizarro took control as governor of Peru.

On June 26, 1541, Governor Pizarro was attacked in his palace by a group of 20 armed men. While trying to pull out his sword, Pizarro was stabbed in the throat. He was buried beneath the floor of the **cathedral** in Lima, Peru.

∼∼∼∼∼∼ FRANCISCO PIZARRO ∼∼∼∼∼∼

Directions: Read each question carefully. Darken the circle for the correct answer.

---

1 After reading the first few paragraphs about Francisco Pizarro, you learn that –

  A his birthday was sometime in the 1460s

  B he served in the Italian military just like his father

  C he was a lot like his cousin Hernando Cortés

  D he sailed to Hispaniola by himself

2 Why was Pizarro interested in traveling to Peru?

  F He wanted to find the shortest and safest route to Asia.

  G He heard that the city was filled with gold.

  H He cared about the Native Americans and wanted to teach them about Christianity.

  J His parents were living there and he wanted to visit them.

3 Punishment in the Inca Empire included all of following <u>except</u> –

  A being thrown off a cliff

  B having your hands cut off

  C being hung up to starve to death

  D being kept in prison for the rest of your life

4 What can you learn from studying the map of Pizarro's first and second expeditions?

  F The first expedition was longer than the second expedition.

  G Both expeditions left from Panama.

  H Colombia is south of Ecuador.

  J Ecuador is north of the equator.

5 What did Pizarro find when he reached the Inca Empire in the Tumbes Region?

  A Hostile Native Americans.

  B An angry emperor who was not interested in visitors.

  C More gold and silver than he had ever seen before.

  D He didn't see anything because the natives would not let him explore their empire.

6 When Pizarro reached Cajamarca, why did the emperor refuse to meet with him?

  F The emperor did not have time for Pizarro.

  G The emperor was not worried about Pizarro and his small army of less than 200 men.

  H The emperor was upset that Pizarro did not bring any gifts with him.

  J The emperor was sick and could not get out of bed.

7 What happened to the Inca emperor after the ransom that Pizarro demanded was paid?

  A Pizarro had the emperor killed.

  B Pizarro returned him safely to the Inca Empire.

  C Pizarro took the emperor back to Spain with him as proof that he had conquered the Inca Empire.

  D Pizarro used the emperor as a slave.

READING

Answers

1 Ⓐ Ⓑ Ⓒ Ⓓ   5 Ⓐ Ⓑ Ⓒ Ⓓ
2 Ⓕ Ⓖ Ⓗ Ⓙ   6 Ⓕ Ⓖ Ⓗ Ⓙ
3 Ⓐ Ⓑ Ⓒ Ⓓ   7 Ⓐ Ⓑ Ⓒ Ⓓ
4 Ⓕ Ⓖ Ⓗ Ⓙ

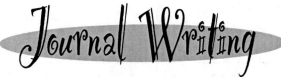

Journal Writing

The date is September 5, 1532. You are a child living in the Tumbes Region of the Inca Empire. You have seen the men of your village huddled around the fire whispering about strange men who have been visiting villages and setting up tents nearby. Late at night, when you are supposed to be sleeping, you have overheard your father talking to your mother about a man and his army wearing fancy clothes and carrying weapons your father has never seen before. You listen as you hear your father tell your mother that the man in charge demanded to see the emperor.

Use your journal to describe what you heard the men around the fire and your parents talking about. How does this make you feel? Will you tell your friends what you heard? What do you think the strange men are planning to do? Are you afraid for your village's safety? Describe what you think is going to happen to you, your village, and your family.

September 5, 1532

Dear Journal,

_____

_____

_____

_____

_____

_____

_____

_____

_____

_____

_____

_____

_____

_____

_____

_____

_____

_____

_____

_____

_____

_____

_____

_____

CABEZA DE VACA

Alvar Núñez Cabeza (cah•VAY•thah) de Vaca (thay•VAH•cah) was born in Spain. His exact birthday isn't known, but most historians agree that he was born in the late 1400s. Very little is known about his early childhood. As a young man, Alvar joined the military.

EXPEDITION TO THE NEW WORLD

In 1527, Cabeza de Vaca left Spain with an expedition to build colonies in North America. During the voyage, a hurricane off the coast of Cuba destroyed the entire fleet of Spanish ships. New ships were sent from Spain. In March 1528, the group of 300 Spaniards landed in present-day Florida near Tampa Bay. The expedition's leader, Pánfilo de Narváez (nah•VAR•ez) claimed the area for Spain.

The expedition was in trouble from the very beginning. The supply ships carrying the group's supplies and **provisions** never arrived. At first, the Native Americans of the Apalachee (ap•uh•LAY•chee) tribe welcomed the **foreigners** into their village. A battle broke out after the Spaniards kidnapped the tribe's leader. Within a short time, the explorers found themselves suffering from strange illnesses and no place to stay. Hungry, they were forced to kill and eat their own horses. By the end of 1528, they had given up. They set sail for Cuba on rafts they made from trees and horse hides.

Once again, a hurricane knocked them off course. A few months later, Cabeza de Vaca, along with an African slave named Esteban, and two other Spaniards arrived half dead on the Texas coast near the present-day city of Galveston. Native Americans of the Karankawa (cair•an•COW•wah) tribe took the four men captive and used them as slaves.

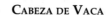

CABEZA DE VACA

In his journal, Cabeza de Vaca wrote that the men of the Karankawa tribe were tall and handsome, but the women did all of the hard work. He observed that they took very good care of their children. If a child died, the tribe would **mourn** for an entire year.

ESCAPE FROM SLAVERY

During his years as a slave, Cabeza de Vaca learned how to heal the sick. The Native Americans believed he was a medicine man. He performed minor surgery and cured diseases with what the Native Americans thought was magic. The Karankawa allowed Cabeza de Vaca to visit other tribes so he could perform his healing ceremonies. It was during one of these trips that Cabeza de Vaca and his men escaped.

JOURNEY ACROSS THE SOUTHWEST

For the next several years, Cabeza de Vaca and the three other men wandered through the American Southwest on foot. Their exact route is unclear, but historians believe they traveled for 2,000 miles across Texas, New Mexico, and Arizona. Walking all day and eating just one small meal in the evening, they came in contact with several Native American tribes that gave the travelers shells, beads, **emerald** arrowheads, and **turquoise**. Cabeza de Vaca wrote about their **adobe** homes and farms of **maize** and beans.

Cabeza de Vaca and his **companions** followed the Gulf of Mexico and the Rio Grande River through New Mexico and into present-day Arizona. In January 1536, they headed south into Mexico. They were hopelessly lost. Amazingly, they were found by Spanish slave traders who took them to San Miguel in New Spain. After living among Native Americans for so many years, Cabeza de Vaca and his men still wore Native American clothing and chose to sleep on the ground instead of in beds.

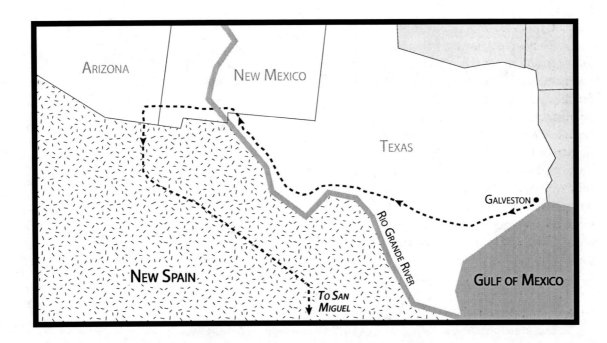

The Seven Cities of Gold

In June 1536, Cabeza de Vaca's group left San Miguel and headed south to Mexico City in New Spain. They had been gone for more than eight years. The friends told wild stories about their adventures. They convinced the Spanish rulers and other Spanish explorers that there were cities of gold located in present-day New Mexico. Native Americans had told Cabeza de Vaca that even the streets in these cities were paved with gold.

Cabeza de Vaca's stories of golden cities sent Spanish explorers north in search of treasure. You will soon learn about famous men like Hernando de Soto (dih•SOH•toh), Father Marcos de Niza, and Francisco Coronado. These explorers risked everything to search for what the Spanish began calling the Seven Cities of Gold.

Governor Cabeza de Vaca

In 1538, Cabeza de Vaca sailed home to Spain. He hoped to return to Florida and the Southwest as the commander of an expedition, but that honor went to Hernando de Soto. Instead, Cabeza de Vaca was appointed governor of a large area of land that is now Paraguay and Argentina.

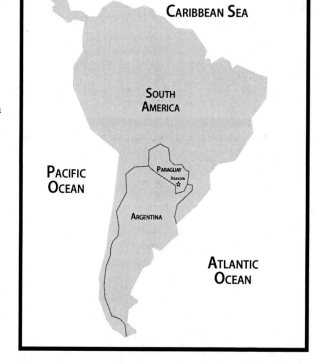

Before taking over as governor, Cabeza de Vaca wrote a best selling book about his adventures. In his book, he wrote about the poor leadership of Pánfilo de Narváez. He blamed Narváez for the deaths of 300 men who made the voyage from Cuba to Florida.

Cabeza de Vaca also wrote about the Native Americans that he met. He was the first explorer to see them as handsome, strong, and intelligent. He wanted to stop the Spanish slave traders from raiding Native American villages and capturing them.

Cabeza de Vaca believed that the Spanish should help the Native Americans rebuild their villages and teach them about Christianity.

From Argentina, Governor Cabeza de Vaca led his soldiers on foot over 1,000 miles of jungles and mountains to rescue Native Americans in Asunción (ah•SOON•see•yawn), the capital of Paraguay. His gentle treatment of the Native Americans angered his soldiers. Governor Cabeza de Vaca wouldn't let them raid the villages or take the Native Americans captive.

In Asunción, Cabeza de Vaca became ill with a fever. He required his soldiers to carry him back to Paraguay on a bed. After arriving in Paraguay, he was removed from office and sent back to Spain in chains. He was found **innocent** of any crime and lived out the rest of his life in Spain.

Name _____

~~~~~~~~~~~~~~~~~ CABEZA DE VACA ~~~~~~~~~~~~~~~~~

Directions: Read each question carefully. Darken the circle for the correct answer.

1. **After reading the first few paragraphs about Cabeza de Vaca, you can conclude that –**

   A he was sent from Spain to build colonies in Cuba

   B he was traveling with a leader who was well organized and knew exactly what he was doing

   C he was lucky to be alive

   D historians aren't sure where he was born

2. **How did Cabeza de Vaca and his group end up in Texas?**

   F They were knocked off course by a hurricane.

   G They walked to Texas from Arizona.

   H They swam across the Gulf of Mexico.

   J They rode to Texas on their horses.

3. **While he was a slave, Cabeza de Vaca learned how to –**

   A grow corn and other vegetables

   B build houses

   C raise pigs

   D heal the sick

4. **What can you learn from studying the map of Cabeza de Vaca's journey across the Southwest?**

   F The explorers crossed the Gulf of Mexico.

   G The journey started in San Miguel.

   H The explorers crossed the Rio Grande River.

   J From Galveston, Texas, the explorers headed east.

5. **According to the map, Texas is –**

   A north of Arizona

   B south of New Spain

   C southeast of New Mexico

   D west of the Rio Grande River

6. **In his best selling book, whom did Cabeza de Vaca blame for the deaths of 300 men who sailed from Cuba to Florida?**

   F Hernando de Soto

   G Himself

   H Native Americans

   J Pánfilo de Narváez

7. **According to the map of South America, which body of water is west of Argentina?**

   A Atlantic Ocean

   B Pacific Ocean

   C Caribbean Sea

   D Gulf of Mexico

8. **After reading about Cabeza de Vaca's treatment of the Native Americans, you get the idea that -**

   F he wanted to have Native American slaves of his own

   G his soldiers did not agree with Cabeza de Vaca's treatment of the Native Americans

   H he wanted to raid their villages

   J he thought they were too weak and stupid to do anything on their own

READING

Answers

1 Ⓐ Ⓑ Ⓒ Ⓓ   5 Ⓐ Ⓑ Ⓒ Ⓓ
2 Ⓕ Ⓖ Ⓗ Ⓙ   6 Ⓕ Ⓖ Ⓗ Ⓙ
3 Ⓐ Ⓑ Ⓒ Ⓓ   7 Ⓐ Ⓑ Ⓒ Ⓓ
4 Ⓕ Ⓖ Ⓗ Ⓙ   8 Ⓕ Ⓖ Ⓗ Ⓙ

MAPPING: CARDINAL AND INTERMEDIATE DIRECTIONS

Geography is the study of the Earth. It includes the Earth's land, water, weather, animal life, and plant life. **Geographers** are people who study geography. Cabeza de Vaca's journey through the Southwest helped him to learn about the land and resources of the area. You can think of yourself as a geographer because you will be learning about important places along Cabeza de Vaca's journey in present-day Arizona, New Mexico, and Texas.

Location is important to the study of geography. It is almost impossible to figure out your location or find your way around if you do not know the four main, or **cardinal directions.** North, south, east, and west are the **cardinal directions**. On a map these directions are labeled N, S, E, and W.

COMPASS ROSE

Between the four main directions are the **intermediate directions.** Northeast, or NE, is the direction between north and east. Southeast, or SE, is the direction between south and east. Southwest, or SW, is the direction between south and west. Northwest, or NW, is the direction between north and west.

A **reference point** is also important for finding your location. A **reference point** is simply a starting point. It's difficult, for example, to travel south if you don't have a starting point.

Example: Carlsbad Caverns National Park is the most popular **tourist** attraction in this state. The huge system of limestone caves contains 30 miles of rooms and hallways that were formed millions of years ago. More than 300,000 Mexican free-tailed bats call the caverns home. Carlsbad Caverns National Park is located <u>south </u>of <u>Capulin Mountain National **Monument.**</u>

This example gives you some very important information. It tells you that your **reference point**, or starting point, will be Capulin Mountain National Monument. Locate Capulin Mountain National Monument on your map of Arizona, New Mexico, and Texas. Put your finger on Capulin Mountain National Monument and slide it <u>south</u>. You should see a picture of Carlsbad Caverns National Park already placed there for you.

Sometimes directions contain more than one **reference point**. Look at the example below:

Example: Alibates (al•ih•BAH•teez) Flint Quarries is the only National Monument in this state. For thousands of years, people came to the red cliffs of the **quarries** in search of **flint**. The rainbow-colored stones found at the Alibates Flint Quarries were used to make fire, tools, and weapons such as arrowheads. The Native Americans could make almost any kind of tool or weapon with flint. Flint is so hard, it can even scratch metal. Alibates Flint Quarries is located <u>southeast</u> of <u>Capulin National Monument</u> and <u>northwest</u> of <u>Fair Park</u>.

This example contains two **reference points** and two sets of directions. They have been underlined for you. Look at your map of Arizona, New Mexico, and Texas. Put your finger on Capulin National Monument and slide it <u>southeast</u>. Since there are many points of interest located southeast, a second **reference point** has been added to help you find your location.

The second **reference point** is Fair Park. Place your finger on Fair Park and slide it <u>northwest</u>. By using both of these **reference points**, you should be able to easily locate Alibates Flint Quarries.

Directions: In this activity you will use reference points, cardinal directions, and intermediate directions to plot important points of interest on a map of present-day Arizona, New Mexico, and Texas, the same states that Cabeza de Vaca traveled through on his journey across the Southwest. Many of these points of interest preserve history. This helps historians learn more about people who lived before us, like Cabeza de Vaca.

1.   Use your coloring pencils to color each of the points of interest on the bottom of the last page.

2.   Use your scissors to carefully cut out each point of interest.

3.   Label the cardinal and intermediate directions on the compass rose drawn for you on the blank map of Arizona, New Mexico, and Texas.

4.   Use the written directions and your compass rose to correctly locate the points of interest on your map.

5.   To get you started, the reference points and directions have been underlined for you in the first five descriptions. You may want to underline the reference points and directions in the rest of the activity.

6.   Glue the symbols in their proper places on your map. (Glue the symbols right over the dots.)

7.   When you are finished placing all of the points of interest, correctly label the states of Arizona, New Mexico, and Texas on your map.

8.   Use your coloring pencils to add color to the rest of your map.

1. Big Thicket National Preserve is special because it has so many different **species** of plants and animals. Visitors see swamps, forests, **plains**, and deserts while exploring Big Thicket National Preserve. Nearly 300 kinds of birds and 1,000 species of flowering plants are protected here. Alligators, frogs, and toads call this preserve home. Big Thicket National Preserve is located <u>southeast</u> of <u>Fair Park</u>.

2. **Petroglyph** (PEH•troe•glif) National Monument contains 17 miles of **mesas** and 25,000 Native American and **Hispanic** images carved on rocks. Petroglyph National Monument is located <u>southwest</u> of <u>Capulin National Monument</u> and <u>northwest</u> of <u>Carlsbad Caverns National Park</u>.

3. Big Bend National Park is one the largest but least visited of America's national parks. There are over 801,000 acres of canyons, mountains, and deserts to explore when visiting Big Bend National Park. The park borders the Rio Grande River for 118 twisting miles. The river flows to the southeast before making a sudden change to the northeast, forming the "big bend" of the Rio Grande. Big Bend National Park is located <u>south</u> of <u>Carlsbad Caverns National Park</u>.

4. San Xavier (ha•vee•AIR) **Mission** was founded by **missionary** Father Kino who worked with Native Americans during the 1700s. San Xavier Mission is known as the "Dove of the Desert" because the painted white walls can be seen from miles around. The mission is still used as a church today. San Xavier Mission is located <u>southwest</u> of <u>Petroglyph National Monument</u>.

5. Painted Desert covers an area of 93,533 acres. The Painted Desert received its name because it contains a wide area of colorful rock **formations**. Water and wind **erosion** continue to change the appearance of the Painted Desert. Painted Desert is located north of San Xavier Mission.

6. San Antonio Missions National Historic Park is a group of four missions built by Spanish missionaries and Native Americans during the 1700s. The four missions, along with the famous Alamo Mission and other nearby villages and forts, came together to form the city of San Antonio. San Antonio Missions National Historic Park is located south of Fair Park.

7. Yuma Territorial Prison State Park preserves the ruins of a prison used from 1876-1910. In 1876, the first seven prisoners entered the Yuma Territorial Prison and were locked into cells that they had helped build themselves. Over the next 33 years, a total of 3,069 prisoners, including 29 women, were locked away in the prison for crimes that ranged from stealing to murder. The prison became so overcrowded that all of the prisoners were moved to a new prison in Florence. The empty building was used as a high school from 1910 to 1914. Over the years, fires, weather, and theft destroyed the prison walls and all of the buildings except the cells, the main gate, and the guard tower. These are left for visitors interested in looking back into prison life more than a hundred years ago. Yuma Territorial State Prison State Park is located northwest of San Xavier Mission and southwest of Painted Desert.

8. Padre Island National Seashore is 113 miles long with over 70 miles of white sand **dunes**, grasslands, and marshes. This **barrier island**, one of the longest in the United States, helps protect the shores of this state from wind and strong storms. Visitors to Padre Island National Seashore discover some of the 350 species of birds native to Padre Island. From late March through July, employees and volunteers search the beaches of Padre Island for nesting sea turtles and their eggs. One of the goals of Padre Island National Seashore is to protect five species of **endangered** sea turtles. Padre Island National Seashore is located southeast of San Antonio Missions Historic Park.

9. Grand Canyon National Park is one of this state's natural wonders. Visitors can journey to the bottom of this 217 mile long, 18 mile wide, one mile deep canyon by walking on foot or riding a mule. At the bottom of the canyon, scientists have found **fossils** of the first living things on Earth. Grand Canyon National Park is located northwest of Painted Desert.

10. Spence Hot Springs is located at the bottom of the Jemez (HAY•mis) Mountains. Underground pockets of boiling water bubble up in pools set among boulders. Spence Hot Springs is located northeast of Painted Desert and west of Capulin Mountain National Monument.

11. Texas Memorial Museum has many things to share about the history of this state. Visitors to the Texas Memorial Museum learn about dinosaurs, gemstones, and rare species of animals. Many historical records and documents about early state history are stored here for everyone to enjoy. Texas Memorial Museum is located northwest of San Antonio Missions Historic Site and southwest of Fair Park.

Big Thicket National Preserve

Petroglyph National Monument

Big Bend National Park

San Xavier Mission

Yuma Territorial Prison State Park

Texas Memorial Museum

San Antonio Missions Historic Park

Painted Desert

Padre Island National Seashore

Grand Canyon National Park

Spence Hot Springs

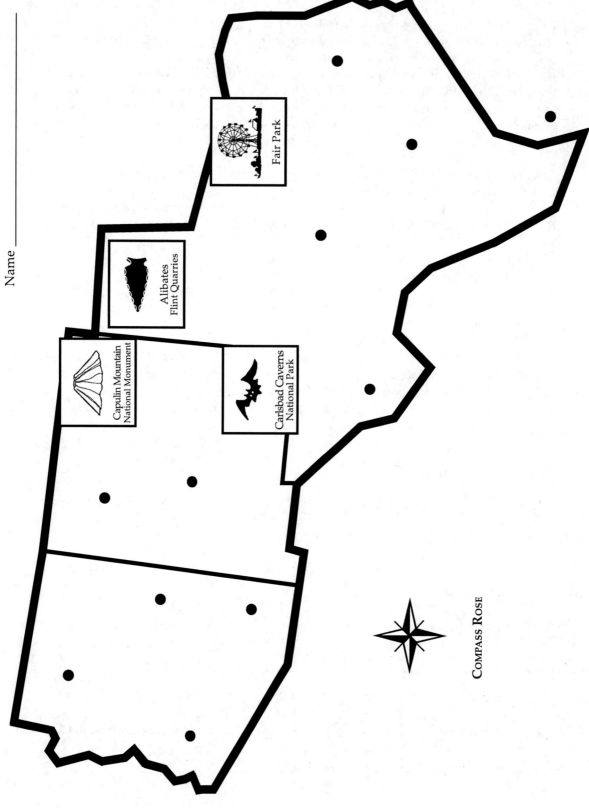

Name _____

Fair Park

Alibates
Flint Quarries

Capulin Mountain
National Monument

Carlsbad Caverns
National Park

COMPASS ROSE

∿∿∿ VOCABULARY QUIZ ∿∿∿

SPANISH EXPLORERS AND CONQUISTADORS
PART IV

Directions: Match the vocabulary word on the left with its definition on the right. Put the letter for the definition on the blank next to the vocabulary word it matches. Use each word and definition only once.

1. _____ anchor

2. _____ turquoise

3. _____ archaeologists

4. _____ tourist

5. _____ architects

6. _____ species

7. _____ artisans

8. _____ quarries

9. _____ captives

10. _____ provisions

11. _____ cathedral

12. _____ plains

13. _____ conflicts

14. _____ innocent

15. _____ culture

16. _____ mourn

17. _____ currents

18. _____ monument

A. scientists who study past human life by looking at prehistoric fossils and tools.

B. a long sandy island that runs next to a shore and provides protection from hurricanes and tidal waves.

C. destruction by wind and rain.

D. not guilty.

E. carving or drawing in rocks usually made by people who lived a long time ago.

F. groups of plants or animals that are alike in many ways.

G. struggles or disagreements.

H. a person sent to spread a religious faith.

I. people who are skilled at making things.

J. mounds of sand that pile up when the wind blows.

K. a person who was originally from Spain.

L. remains of plants or animals preserved in earth or rock.

M. a person who travels for pleasure.

N. supplies of food taken on a trip.

O. quickly moving bodies of water.

P. entered an area and took it over by force.

Q. arrangements of something.

19. _____ textiles

20. _____ barrier island

21. _____ invaded

22. _____ companions

23. _____ harvest

24. _____ dunes

25. _____ fleet

26. _____ erosion

27. _____ equator

28. _____ emerald

29. _____ flint

30. _____ maize

31. _____ endangered

32. _____ missionary

33. _____ foreigners

34. _____ fossils

35. _____ mission

36. _____ formations

37. _____ adobe

38. _____ petroglyph

39. _____ mesas

40. _____ Hispanic

R.   fabrics made from weaving or knitting yarn.

S.   pick crops.

T.   a bluish green stone that turns bright blue when polished.

U.   a valuable green colored stone that is often used in jewelry.

V.   in danger of disappearing forever.

W.   people who are held without permission.

X.   wide treeless areas of land.

Y.   people from another country or nation.

Z.   large group of ships.

AA. a heavy clay used for making bricks.

BB. a group of people with a shared set of beliefs, goals, religious customs, attitudes, and social practices.

CC. a very hard stone that makes a spark when struck by steel.

DD. building, stone, or statue created to remember a person or event.

EE. open pits that provide stones for building.

FF. the invisible line that cuts through the center of the Earth from east to west.

GG. church.

HH. steep hills with flat tops.

II. a large important church, usually the church of a bishop.

JJ. to feel and express deep sadness.

KK. people who design buildings.

LL. corn.

MM. friends.

NN. secure a boat so it won't float away.

HERNANDO DE SOTO

Hernando de Soto (dih•SOH•toh) was born in Spain. The exact date of his birth is unknown, but many historians believe it was 1500. As a young man growing up, Hernando heard wild stories from explorers who had reached the New World to find fame and fortune. This was the kind of life that Hernando wanted for himself.

ARRIVAL IN THE NEW WORLD

Hernando de Soto was only 14 or 15 years old when he traveled to the New World for the first time. In 1515, he was with famous conquistador (con•KEE•stah•dor) Vasco Núñez de Balboa when he raided a Native American village in Panama. His **brutality** and surprise attacks on Native American villages before the sun came up earned Hernando de Soto the title "Child of the Sun."

In 1530, Hernando de Soto led his first expedition in the New World. He sailed up the coast of the **Yucatán Peninsula**, searching for a shorter water route to Asia. Unfortunately for Hernando de Soto and hundreds of other explorers, a shorter route to Asia did not exist.

CONQUERING THE INCA EMPIRE

In 1532, Hernando de Soto helped Francisco Pizarro (puh•ZAR•roh) conquer the Inca Empire. De Soto sailed his own ships and brought an army of men with him. Upon arrival in Peru, Pizarro immediately made Hernando de Soto one of his captains.

During the famous Battle of Cajamarca (cah•ha•MAR•cah), Hernando de Soto was in charge of three groups of soldiers who **ambushed** the Inca Empire on horseback, killing thousands, and taking the emperor captive. After the battle, Hernando de Soto and his men raided the village. They took as much gold and silver as they could carry. The Incas gathered two rooms of silver and one room of gold to pay for the safe return of their emperor. Pizarro and de Soto took the treasure, but murdered the emperor anyway. De Soto and his army followed Pizarro to the Incan capital of Cuzco (COOZ•coh). They invaded Cuzco and completely defeated the Inca Empire.

GOVERNOR DE SOTO

  Hernando de Soto returned to Spain a very wealthy man. He had achieved his dream of fame and fortune. De Soto could have lived the rest of his life as one of Spain's richest men. Instead, he asked the king of Spain for permission to explore the South Sea. Remember, the South Sea, known today as the Pacific Ocean, was discovered by Spanish explorer Vasco Núñez Balboa in 1513.

  The king of Spain had bigger plans for Hernando de Soto. Cabeza (cah•VAY•thah) de Vaca (thay•VAH•cah) had just returned to Mexico City with news about the Seven Cities of Gold in the New World. The king appointed de Soto as governor of Cuba.

  As governor, Hernando de Soto was expected to search for the golden cities and build permanent colonies in North America for Spain. He was given four years to complete the project.

HERNANDO DE SOTO

ARRIVING IN FLORIDA

  Hernando de Soto selected 620 young and eager Spanish and Portuguese volunteers. Soon after arriving in Cuba, they sailed west toward North America in nine ships with weapons, equipment, and more than 500 horses, mules, pigs, and other types of **livestock**. De Soto planned to colonize North America, explore the continent for the Seven Cities of Gold, and search for a water route to Asia.

  In May 1539, Hernando de Soto and his nine ships landed at Charlotte Harbor in present-day Florida. Priests, craftsmen, **engineers**, farmers, and merchants traveled with Hernando de Soto. The people he brought with him came from Cuba, Europe, and Africa. This was the first time that many of these people had ever traveled away from their homes.

JOURNEY THROUGH THE SOUTHEAST

A month after arriving in Florida, Hernando de Soto and his men traveled north on horseback. They explored Florida's west coast. Archaeologists (ar•kee•OL•uh•jists) have found proof that de Soto spent his first winter in Florida's **panhandle**, near the present-day city of Tallahassee.

In the spring of 1540, de Soto led an expedition through the present-day Southeast region of the United States. The group traveled through the states of Georgia, South Carolina, North Carolina, Tennessee, and Alabama. They planned to head south toward the Gulf of Mexico and meet a ship with supplies, but they were ambushed by a Native American tribe. De Soto was forced to escape north toward the Tennessee River.

De Soto claimed all of the land in the Southeast region for Spain. Along the way, his troops searched for gold and battled Native American warriors who didn't want de Soto and his men crossing through their territory. As he did in Peru, de Soto captured Native American chiefs and held them for ransom. If the ransom wasn't paid, de Soto and his men raided their villages, stealing food and kidnapping Native American women.

LAKE MICHIGAN

De Soto's journey through the Southeast was dangerous. The battles didn't always go well for de Soto and his men. By the spring of 1541, they had traveled through Kentucky, Indiana, and Illinois. They discovered Lake Michigan, one of the five **Great Lakes**, but no golden cities or water route to Asia. De Soto's army was wounded, sick, and surrounded by enemies. In addition, they had lost most of their weapons and horses.

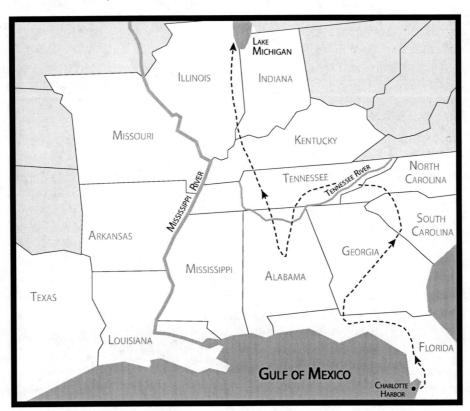

DISCOVERING THE MISSISSIPPI RIVER

In May, de Soto's troops headed south through Illinois. On May 8, 1541, they reached the Mississippi River. Instead of celebrating the discovery of such an important waterway, de Soto was angry that he and his 400 men had to cross the wide river. The fact that the river was constantly guarded by hostile Native Americans made crossing even more difficult. De Soto and his men spent more than a month building rafts. After safely crossing the Mississippi River, they continued traveling through present-day Missouri, Arkansas, Texas, and Louisiana. After claiming all of the land for Spain, they spent the winter along the Arkansas River.

SICKNESS AND DEATH

In the spring of 1542, Hernando de Soto became very ill with a fever. He died from his illness on May 21, 1542. To keep his death a secret, de Soto's men wrapped his body in a cloth and dumped it into the Mississippi River. His army escaped south to the safety of Mexico City in New Spain. De Soto's expedition had not produced any gold or a shorter route to Asia. Hostile Native Americans made it too dangerous to build colonies. Without permanent settlements or colonists to defend Spain's land, explorers from other countries could claim the land for themselves.

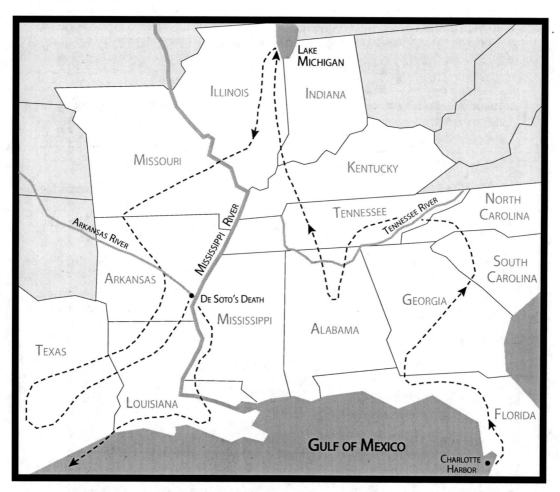

~~~~~ Hernando de Soto ~~~~~

Directions: Read each question carefully. Darken the circle for the correct answer.

1 Hernando de Soto was known as "Child of the Sun" because –

   A he was born in sunny Spain

   B he slept during the day and traveled at night

   C he led brutal attacks on Native Americans before the sun came up

   D he enjoyed swimming and laying out in the sun

2 Which statement about Hernando de Soto is <u>true</u>?

   F He never made it to the New World.

   G He helped Francisco Pizarro conquer the Inca Empire.

   H He wasn't interested in finding a shorter water route to Asia

   J Francisco Pizarro didn't want Hernando de Soto's help.

3 Between 1515 and 1539, which event in Hernando de Soto's life came <u>first</u>?

   A He sailed up the coast of the Yucatán Peninsula.

   B He arrived in Florida.

   C He raided a Native American village in Panama.

   D He returned to Spain a very wealthy man.

4 After arriving in Florida, de Soto planned to do all of the following <u>except</u> –

   F show kindness to the Native Americans

   G build colonies in North America

   H find the Seven Cities of Gold

   J search for a water route to Asia

5 According to the definition in the Glossary, which of the following is <u>not</u> one of the five Great Lakes?

   A Lake Michigan

   B Lake Ontario

   C Lake Superior

   D Lake Illinois

6 Which of the following is an example of a <u>primary source</u>?

   F A feather from the hat that Hernando de Soto wore.

   G A movie about conquistadors featuring a character who plays Hernando de Soto.

   H A museum display of the types of coins that might have been used to pay the Incan emperor's ransom.

   J Hernando de Soto's biography.

7 What can you learn by studying the maps of Hernando de Soto's journey through the Southeast?

   A The journey started in the Atlantic Ocean.

   B After reaching Lake Michigan, the explorers headed east.

   C De Soto and his men crossed the Mississippi River in Tennessee.

   D De Soto's journey crossed through the southwest corner of Indiana.

READING

Answers

1 Ⓐ Ⓑ Ⓒ Ⓓ   5 Ⓐ Ⓑ Ⓒ Ⓓ
2 Ⓕ Ⓖ Ⓗ Ⓙ   6 Ⓕ Ⓖ Ⓗ Ⓙ
3 Ⓐ Ⓑ Ⓒ Ⓓ   7 Ⓐ Ⓑ Ⓒ Ⓓ
4 Ⓕ Ⓖ Ⓗ Ⓙ

A time line is a tool used to list dates and events in the order that they happened. The time line below lists important dates in Hernando de Soto's life. Notice that many of the events are missing.

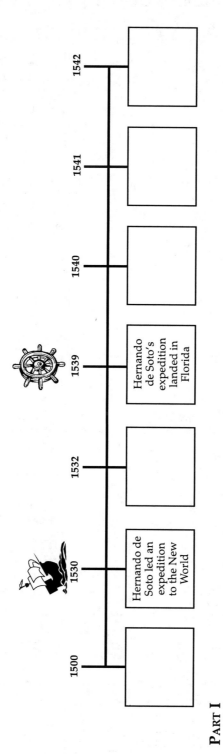

| 1500 | 1530 | 1532 | 1539 | 1540 | 1541 | 1542 |

Hernando de Soto led an expedition to the New World

Hernando de Soto's expedition landed in Florida

PART I

Directions: In the first part of this activity, you will use your information about Hernando de Soto to cut out and glue the missing events into the time line. Then, choose the picture that you think best represents each event. Color and cut out each picture before gluing it into its proper spot on the time line. Since you weren't there for any of these events, this time line would be considered a **secondary source**.

| Hernando de Soto helped conquer the Inca Empire | Hernando de Soto discovered Lake Michigan | De Soto's body was dumped in the Mississippi River | Hernando de Soto was born in Spain | Hernando de Soto led an expedition through the Southeast |

PART II

Directions: In the second part of this activity, you will create a time line of someone else's life by listing the dates and events in order as they happened. Choose someone outside of your class: a parent, a grandparent, a friend, or another relative. Since this person will be supplying the information about his or her own life, this time line would be considered a **primary source**.

1. Use the boxes drawn to make a time line of someone else's life. Put the dates in the top boxes and the events in the bottom boxes.

2. The first date of the time line should be the person's birth. The last date should be the most recent event in his or her life.

3. Try to list only the important events. If you need more room, you may add more boxes on the back.

4. On a separate piece of paper choose one of the events from the time line and draw a picture of it.

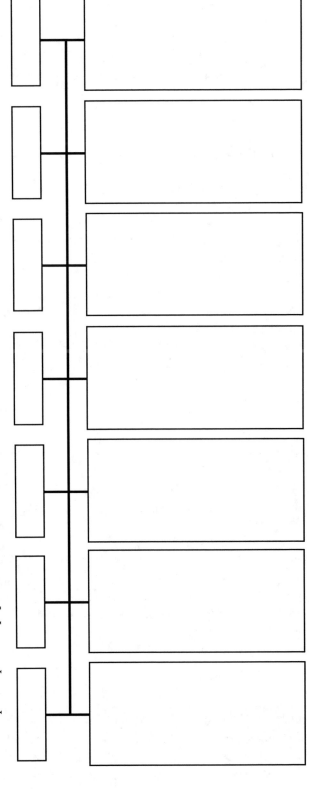

FRANCISCO DE CORONADO

Francisco Vázquez de Coronado was born in Spain in 1510. He was born into a noble Spanish family and was well educated. In 1535, Coronado traveled to the New World. Within three years of his arrival in Mexico City, Coronado had married the daughter of a colonial **treasurer**, stopped a slave **rebellion**, and was appointed governor of an important province in New Spain.

Governor Coronado had heard about Cabeza de Vaca's journey across the American Southwest and the Seven Cities of Gold. More than anything, he wanted to discover the golden cities and become rich and famous.

FATHER MARCOS DE NIZA

Governor Coronado was an important man in New Spain. He couldn't simply leave and go exploring based on stories that might or might not be true. In 1539, Father Marcos de Niza was sent to **investigate** Cabeza de Vaca's story about the Seven Cities of Gold.

Father Marcos de Niza led a group that was guided by Esteban, the same African slave who had traveled with Cabeza de Vaca. Esteban traveled ahead of the group. He promised that if he found gold, he would send back a messenger carrying a wooden cross. If the cross was big, it meant that Esteban had discovered a large amount of gold.

FRANCISCO CORONADO

Esteban was gone for a long period of time. Finally, a messenger returned to the group carrying a wooden cross that was six feet tall. Knowing this meant a large amount of gold had been found, Marcos de Niza and his group of explorers rushed to catch up with Esteban. They soon discovered that the people who lived in the golden cities had killed Esteban. Father Marcos de Niza planted the cross in the hill above the Seven Cities of Gold and claimed the area for Spain. He rushed back to Mexico City to tell of his discoveries.

JOURNEY TO THE SEVEN CITIES OF GOLD

Governor Coronado had the proof that he needed. In 1540, he gathered an army of more than 1,000 people. The group included Spanish soldiers, Native American slaves, and missionaries. They brought along horses and herds of sheep, pigs, and cattle. Father Marcos de Niza guided the group north from New Spain through the mountain ranges of present-day Arizona and New Mexico in search of the Seven Cities of Gold.

Upon arrival, Coronado found Native Americans of the Zuñi tribe living in a town. Coronado thought the Zuñi people were guarding the town's golden treasures. Governor Coronado commanded his army to attack.

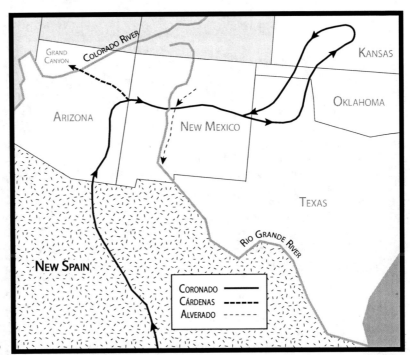

The Zuñi people fought to defend their village. Coronado almost lost his life during the bloody battle. In the end, Coronado and his men defeated the Zuñi people and took over the town.

Francisco Coronado expected to find treasures of gold inside the Zuñi village. He found no such thing. The Seven Cities of Gold turned out to be a **hoax**. Still, Coronado was certain that gold could be found in the Southwest. He set up camp in northern New Mexico and sent small groups of men in search of gold.

CORONADO'S OTHER EXPEDITIONS

Gold seekers led by Lopez de Cárdenas (CAR•the•nahs) were sent west all the way to the Colorado River on the border between California and Arizona. They were disappointed that they could not get into the Colorado River because it was at the bottom of a very deep canyon. Cárdenas and his group didn't realize it at the time, but they were the first explorers to see the Grand Canyon in Arizona.

Hernando de Alverado was sent south and followed the Rio Grande River through New Mexico where he saw great herds of buffalo. Coronado himself led an expedition east through the present-day states of Texas, Oklahoma, and Kansas. These explorers found thousands of Native Americans, but no gold.

In 1542, Francisco Coronado returned to Mexico City in New Spain. He felt like a complete failure because he had not found any gold. We consider him a success because he explored and made the first maps of the Southwest. He also claimed a large area of land for Spain.

≈≈≈≈≈ FRANCISCO DE CORONADO ≈≈≈≈≈

Directions: Read each question carefully. Darken the circle for the correct answer.

1   After reading the first two paragraphs about Francisco de Coronado, you learn that –

   A   he wasn't interested in wealth or fame

   B   he was never married

   C   he was born into a poor family that didn't value education

   D   he did many things in a short amount of time

2   Coronado was born in 1510 and traveled to the New World in 1535. How old was Coronado when he arrived in the New World?

   F   35

   G   65

   H   25

   J   15

3   In 1539, Father Marcos de Niza was sent to investigate Cabeza de Vaca's story about the Seven Cities of Gold. Another word for <u>investigate</u> is –

   A   ignore

   B   navigate

   C   examine

   D   conquer

4   What happened to Esteban, the African slave who traveled with Marcos de Niza?

   F   He ran away.

   G   He found the water route to Asia.

   H   He was killed.

   J   He returned safely to the group and told them about the gold he had found.

5   What can you learn by studying the map of Coronado's journey to the Seven Cities of Gold?

   A   Coronado's journey started west of the Rio Grande River.

   B   After arriving in Arizona, the explorers headed south.

   C   Coronado and his men never traveled through Texas.

   D   Coronado was forced to cross the Mississippi River.

6   According to the map, the Grand Canyon is located –

   F   south of New Spain

   G   northeast of the Rio Grande River

   H   north of Kansas

   J   in the northwest corner of Arizona

7   What did Coronado find inside the Seven Cities of Gold?

   A   Gold

   B   Native American villages

   C   The Grand Canyon

   D   Silver

8   Lopez de Cárdenas was the first to see -

   F   New Mexico

   G   the Rio Grande River

   H   the Gulf of Mexico

   J   the Grand Canyon

Answers   READING

1   Ⓐ Ⓑ Ⓒ Ⓓ   5   Ⓐ Ⓑ Ⓒ Ⓓ
2   Ⓕ Ⓖ Ⓗ Ⓙ   6   Ⓕ Ⓖ Ⓗ Ⓙ
3   Ⓐ Ⓑ Ⓒ Ⓓ   7   Ⓐ Ⓑ Ⓒ Ⓓ
4   Ⓕ Ⓖ Ⓗ Ⓙ   8   Ⓕ Ⓖ Ⓗ Ⓙ

MAPPING: LATITUDE AND LONGITUDE

Using a map is a skill that must be learned and practiced. You live in a house or an apartment that has an exact address. The number on your house, your apartment number, your street name, and your zip code are all part of your address. No other house or apartment in the world has the same exact address as your house or apartment. If the post office, fire department, or your friends need to find you, they use your address.

Just like your house or apartment, every place on Earth has an exact location or address that can be written in numbers. Instead of street names and apartment numbers, these places on Earth use lines of **latitude** and **longitude**.

LINES OF LATITUDE

Lines of **latitude**, or parallels, are lines drawn on a map to show how far north or south a place is from the **equator**. The equator is the invisible line that runs from east to west through the center of the Earth. Latitude lines also run from east to west. Those latitude lines that appear above the equator are known as **north latitude** lines. Those latitude lines that appear below the equator are known as **south latitude** lines.

Each line of north and south latitude is measured in degrees. The equator is 0°. The lines above the equator are 1°N (north) to 80°N (north). The lines below the equator are 1°S (south) to 80°S (south).

LINES OF LONGITUDE

Lines of **longitude**, or meridians, are lines drawn on a map to show how far east or west a place is from the **prime meridian**. The prime meridian is an invisible line that runs from north to south through the center of the Earth. Longitude lines also run from north to south. Those longitude lines that appear on the right side of the prime meridian are known as **east longitude** lines. Those longitude lines that appear on the left side of the prime meridian are known as **west longitude** lines.

Like the lines of latitude, each line of east and west longitude is also measured in degrees. The prime meridian is 0°. The lines to the right of the prime meridian are 1°E (east) to 180°E (east). The lines to the left of the prime meridian are 1°W (west) to 180°W (west).

• Lines of **latitude** and **longitude** come together on a map to form a grid. This makes it easy to find any place in the world if you know the latitude and longitude address.

For Example:

To find a place on the map below that has the address 40°N, 100°W, follow these steps:

1. Find the place where the equator and the prime meridian cross. Put your finger on that spot. Remember, those lines on a map are always 0°.
2. The first part of the address is 40°N. Since you are looking for a place that is north, you would look at the latitude lines that are above the equator. Slide your finger up (or north) to the line labeled 40°.
3. The other part of the address is 100°W. Since you are looking for a place that is west, you would look at the longitude lines that are left of the prime meridian. Slide your finger left (or west) to the line labeled 100°.
4. On an actual map of the world, you would be in the middle of the United States!

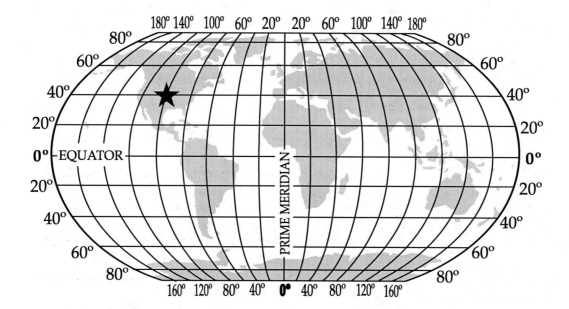

In this activity, you will use lines of **latitude** and **longitude** to find an exact location and plot points of interest on a map of the states that Francisco Coronado and his men traveled through in search of the Seven Cities of Gold. Many of these present-day points of interest preserve history. Remember, preserving pieces of our past helps historians learn more about the people who lived before us.

EXAMPLE: Oklahoma City is the largest city and capital of Oklahoma. There are more than 5,000 oil wells within 60 miles of this city. Oklahoma City is located at 35°N, 97°W.

Follow these steps to find Oklahoma City on your map.

1.   Before you begin, notice that all of the latitude lines on your map are labeled N (north). All of the longitude lines are labeled W (west). This is because Arizona, Kansas, New Mexico, Oklahoma, and Texas all lie above the equator, or north, and left of the prime meridian, or west.

     • You don't actually see the equator or the prime meridian on this map because the map has been made bigger so you can easily work with it. Look at a globe in your classroom to see if these states actually lie north of the equator and west of the prime meridian.

2.   Find the latitude line labeled 35°N. Since every latitude line on this map is 2° apart, 35°N will be found between 34°N and 36°N. Put your finger in this space.

3.   Slide your finger along 35°N until you come to the longitude line labeled 97°W. Since every longitude line on this map is 2° apart, 97°W will be found between 96°W and 98°W.

4.   This is the exact address for Oklahoma City. You should see a star representing the capital city already placed there for you.

Directions:

1. Use your scissors to carefully cut out the points of interest on the bottom of the last page.

2. Use the latitude and longitude addresses below to glue the points of interest in their proper locations on the blank map.

3. When you are finished placing all of the points of interest, neatly label each state with its name.

4. Use your coloring pencils to add color to your map.

~~~~~~

1. Tuzigoot National Monument preserves 800 year old ruins of the Sinagua (see•NAH•gwah) people. The village included two and three story buildings where 200 Native Americans once lived. The Sinagua were farmers who often traveled hundreds of miles to trade with other Native American groups. Tuzigoot National Monument is located at 34°N, 111°W.

2. Pecos was the home of the world's first rodeo in 1883. Today it is the site of the Texas Rodeo Hall of Fame. Pecos is located at 31°N, 104°W.

3. Boot Hill Museum preserves the history of Dodge City and the Old West. Dodge City was founded in 1865, as a stopping place for **pioneers** traveling West along the Santa Fe Trail. By 1872, Dodge City was the world's largest shipping point for longhorn cattle. More than 20,000 **artifacts** are on display at the museum. Boot Hill Museum is located at 39°N, 101°W.

4. Monument Valley is located on the Navajo (nah•VUH•hoe) Reservation. Erosion has caused interesting rock formations. They have names like Rooster Rock, Totem Pole, Elephant Rock, and Three Sisters. Monument Valley is located at 36°N, 110°W.

5. Boca Chica State Park is a great place to get away from it all. Its location on Boca Chica Beach offers visitors swimming, camping, fishing, and bird watching opportunities. Boca Chica State Park is located at 28°N, 99°W.

6. Angelina National Forest is one of four national forests tucked in the eastern part of this state. The lakes and rivers in the Angelina National Forest are very popular places for fishing, boating, and water skiing. Angelina National Forest is located at 31°N, 95°W.

7. Fort Davis National Historic Site was built to protect travelers, mail coaches, and freight wagons making their way toward the California Gold Rush in the 1850s. There are 24 historic buildings and over 100 ruins for visitors to explore at Fort Davis. Fort Davis is located at 31°N, 101°W.

8. Aztec Ruins National Monument protects the remains of the Anasazi (ahn•uh•SAH•zee) who built one of the largest **pueblo** communities in this area. Aztec Ruins is located at 36°N, 107°W.

9. Gila (HEE•luh) Cliff Dwellings National Monument features cliff dwellings carved by the Mogollon (MOE•gee•yahn) people hundreds of years ago. Gila Cliff Dwelling National Monument is located at 33°N, 108°W.

10. Kitt Peak National **Observatory** is on the Papago Reservation. Visitors can take guided tours of the observatory during the day or gaze at the stars with the observatory's night programs. Kitt Peak is located at 32°N, 111°W.

11. Palo Duro Canyon State Park is known as this state's "Grand Canyon." The canyon is 120 miles long, 20 miles wide, and 800 feet deep. Palo Duro Canyon State Park is located at 35°N, 102°W.

12. Dinosaur Valley State Park contains some of the best preserved dinosaur tracks in the world. The giant footprints are located in a riverbed. Visitors to Dinosaur Valley State Park also enjoy camping, hiking, swimming, and mountain biking. Dinosaur Valley State Park is located at 32°N, 98°W.

13. Living Desert State Park allows visitors to take a walking tour and view mountain lions, bobcats, golden eagles, roadrunners, prairie dogs, and other animals in their natural **habitats**. Living Desert States Park is located at 33°N, 104°W.

14. Fort Larned National Historic Site was once a military fort built to protect pioneers who were headed West on the Santa Fe Trail. Soldiers at Fort Larned protected travelers and mail coaches while maintaining friendly relationships with Native Americans. Fort Larned National Historic Site is located at 39°N, 98°W.

15. Cherokee Heritage Center tells the story of the Cherokee people through the Cherokee National Museum. Exhibits include art shows, pottery demonstrations, and storytelling. Cherokee Heritage Center is located at 36°N, 95°W.

Kitt Peak Observatory

Dinosaur Valley State Park

Aztec Ruins

Angelina National Forest

Palo Duro Canyon State Park

Fort Davis National Historic Site

Gila Cliff Dwellings National Monument

Pecos

Tuzigoot National Monument

Monument Valley

Cherokee Heritage Center

Boca Chica State Park

Boot Hill Museum

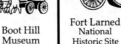
Fort Larned National Historic Site

Living Desert State Park

Name _____

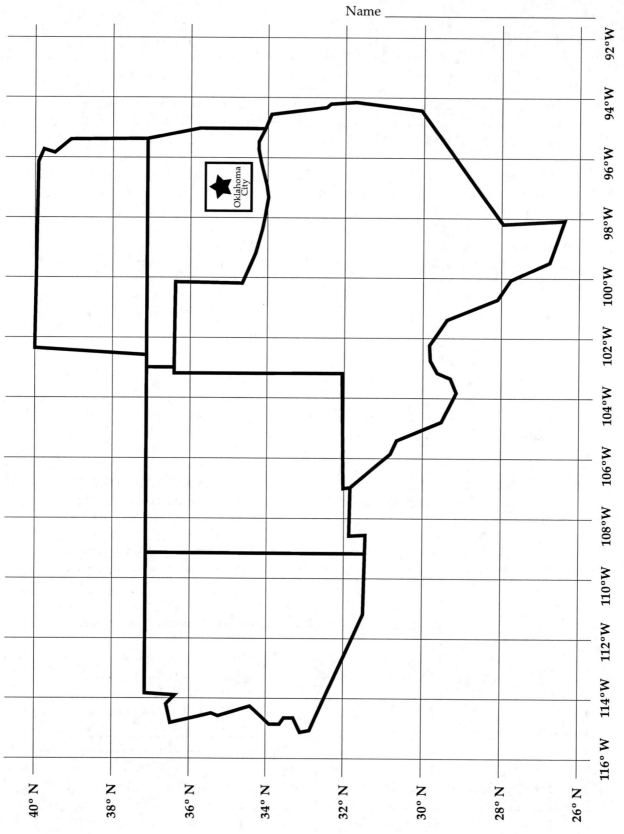

★ Oklahoma City

92°W
94°W
96°W
98°W
100°W
102°W
104°W
106°W
108°W
110°W
112°W
114°W
116°W

40° N
38° N
36° N
34° N
32° N
30° N
28° N
26° N

JUAN CABRILLO

Juan Rodríguez Cabrillo (cah•BREE•yo) was born in the late 1400s. Historians aren't sure of his exact date of birth or whether he was born in Portugal (POR•chuw•gal) or Spain. Most agree that he was born of poor parents and worked for a ship builder in Spain.

CONQUERING THE AZTEC EMPIRE

As a young man, Juan left his home in Spain and sailed to Cuba. In 1519, he sailed to Mexico and helped Hernando Cortés conquer the Aztec Empire. Cabrillo was in command of a group of soldiers who fought the Aztecs with **crossbows**.

After the defeat of the Aztecs, Cabrillo joined other Spanish military expeditions in present-day southern Mexico, Guatemala, and San Salvador. He finally settled in Guatemala.

As a reward for his military service, the king of Spain gave Cabrillo huge areas of land that could be used for mining and farming. He was also permitted to capture Native Americans and use them as slaves to help him with his projects.

WEALTHY CONQUISTADOR

By the 1530s, Juan Cabrillo had become a leading citizen of Santiago, Guatemala's largest town. Using a port on Guatemala's Pacific coast, Cabrillo established a trade business that imported and **exported** goods between Guatemala, Spain, and other parts of the New World.

JUAN CABRILLO

The ships for Cabrillo's business were built in Guatemala by Native American slaves. Cabrillo's well built ships were used by Spain to explore the Pacific Ocean. Cabrillo's trade business and his skills in mining gold made him one of the richest conquistadors in Mexico.

EXPLORING THE PACIFIC OCEAN

In 1540, Juan Cabrillo was asked to lead an expedition to explore the Pacific Ocean. Cabrillo had big plans for his expedition. He hoped to find the famous Seven Cities of Gold and a water route connecting the Atlantic and Pacific oceans together.

On June 24, 1542, the Cabrillo expedition sailed from the port in present-day Acapulco. He took three ships with a crew of sailors, soldiers, Native American and black slaves, merchants, a priest, livestock, and enough supplies for two years.

CALIFORNIA

After sailing for more than 100 days, Cabrillo's ships entered what he described as a "closed and very good **harbor**." He claimed the harbor for Spain and named it San Miguel. Today, this harbor is known as San Diego Bay.

Cabrillo's crew spent the next three months exploring the coast of present-day California. They visited Santa Catalina Island and Monterey Bay. Some historians believe that Cabrillo may have sailed as far north as Oregon.

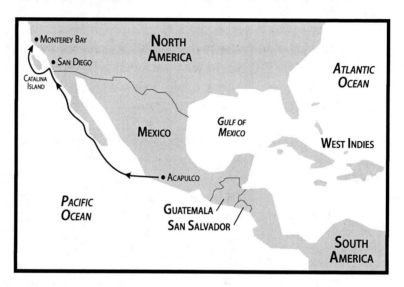

CABRILLO'S DEATH AND LEGACY

Bad weather forced Cabrillo and his crew to return to San Miguel and spend the winter. During this time, Cabrillo stumbled on a jagged rock. It's not clear whether Cabrillo simply fell or got into a fight with Native Americans. The fall broke his leg and Cabrillo developed **gangrene**. On January 3, 1543, Juan Cabrillo died from his injury. In the spring, his crew tried again to sail north. Wind and strong ocean currents forced them to return to Mexico.

Juan Cabrillo's expedition failed to find the Seven Cities of Gold or a water route connecting the Pacific and Atlantic oceans. Of course, you know that neither of these ever existed. The Atlantic and Pacific oceans have always been separated by land. The Seven Cities of Gold were actually villages of Zuñi people and no gold was ever found.

Cabrillo's expedition did give Spain its first look at the west coast of North America. He also claimed new land for Spain and is remembered as the first European to explore the coast of California. Many streets and buildings in present-day California are named after Juan Cabrillo.

~~~~ JUAN CABRILLO ~~~~

Directions: Read each question carefully. Darken the circle for the correct answer.

1   **Most historians agree that Juan Cabrillo –**

   A   was born in the early 1400s

   B   worked for a silk merchant

   C   grew up poor

   D   was born in England

2   **After helping Hernando Cortés conquer the Aztec Empire, Juan Cabrillo settled in –**

   F   Mexico

   G   Spain

   H   San Salvador

   J   Guatemala

3   **Who helped Juan Cabrillo with his trade business?**

   A   Hernando Cortés

   B   Native American slaves

   C   The king of Spain

   D   Other Spanish conquistadors

4   **What was Juan Cabrillo hoping to find when he led an expedition to explore the Pacific Ocean?**

   F   The Mississippi River

   G   The Gulf of Mexico

   H   The Seven Cities of Gold

   J   California

5   **What did Juan Cabrillo find instead?**

   A   The Mississippi River

   B   The Gulf of Mexico

   C   The Seven Cities of Gold

   D   California

6   **What did Juan Cabrillo name the harbor that we call the San Diego Bay?**

   F   San Miguel

   G   Monterey Bay

   H   Catalina Island

   J   San Salvador

7   **What can you learn from studying Juan Cabrillo's route through the Pacific Ocean?**

   A   His journey started in Guatemala.

   B   From Acapulco, Juan Cabrillo sailed east.

   C   After reaching Catalina Island, Juan Cabrillo traveled north.

   D   Juan Cabrillo's expedition ended in San Salvador.

8   **According to the map, Guatemala is –**

   F   southeast of San Salvador

   G   north of Mexico

   H   southwest of the West Indies

   J   in the Gulf of Mexico

9   **Between 1540 and 1543, which event happened <u>last</u>?**

   A   Juan Cabrillo sailed from Acapulco.

   B   Juan Cabrillo stumbled on a rock.

   C   Juan Cabrillo explored the coast of California.

   D   Juan Cabrillo visited Catalina Island and Monterey Bay.

READING

Answers

1 Ⓐ Ⓑ Ⓒ Ⓓ   6 Ⓕ Ⓖ Ⓗ Ⓙ

2 Ⓕ Ⓖ Ⓗ Ⓙ   7 Ⓐ Ⓑ Ⓒ Ⓓ

3 Ⓐ Ⓑ Ⓒ Ⓓ   8 Ⓕ Ⓖ Ⓗ Ⓙ

4 Ⓕ Ⓖ Ⓗ Ⓙ   9 Ⓐ Ⓑ Ⓒ Ⓓ

5 Ⓐ Ⓑ Ⓒ Ⓓ

FIND THE FIB

During the 1400s and 1500s, the first Spanish explorers and conquistadors made voyages to the New World. You have learned how they claimed new land for Spain, searched for golden treasures, and defeated Native Americans who stood in the way of their progress. In this activity, you will collect facts about one of these famous men to make a game called "Find the Fib."

Directions:

1. Pick a Spanish explorer or conquistador to make the game "Find the Fib." Choose from Christopher Columbus, Amerigo Vespucci, Vasco de Balboa, Juan Ponce de León, Ferdinand Magellan, Hernando Cortés, Francisco Pizarro, Cabeza de Vaca, Hernando de Soto, Francisco Coronado, or Juan Cabrillo.

2. Use your scissors to cut apart the "Find the Fib" cards given to you by your teacher. You will need 20 cards.

3. Use **primary** and **secondary** sources that include the information you have read, encyclopedias, books in the library, and the Internet to find 15 true facts about the Spanish explorer or conquistador you have chosen.

4. Write each fact on a separate card. It's important to fit the whole fact on one side of the card.

5. Make up 5 false facts, or "fibs" about your explorer or conquistador. Make each fib as believable as possible so that it can't be easily seen as a fib.

6. Write each fib on a separate card, just like you did with the true facts. Again, it's important to fit the whole fib on one side of the card.

7. Decorate the blank side of each card with a design or picture to represent your Spanish explorer or conquistador. Your teacher will give you pictures of the explorers and conquistadors for you to color and glue onto your cards. Of course, you may also draw and color your own pictures.

8. Mix and shuffle all of the cards together, so the true facts and fibs are mixed together.

9. Number the cards 1-20.

10. Make an answer key for yourself so you will know which cards are the true facts and which cards are the fibs.

11. Give your cards to 2 or 3 other people in the class to see if they can find the true facts and the fibs.

SAMPLE CARD

FRONT	BACK

1

In 1519, Juan Cabrillo sailed to Mexico and helped Hernando Cortés conquer the Aztec Empire.

FIND THE FIB CARDS

FIND THE FIB EXPLORERS AND CONQUISTADORS

CHRISTOPHER COLUMBUS CHRISTOPHER COLUMBUS CHRISTOPHER COLUMBUS CHRISTOPHER COLUMBUS CHRISTOPHER COLUMBUS

AMERIGO VESPUCCI AMERIGO VESPUCCI AMERIGO VESPUCCI AMERIGO VESPUCCI AMERIGO VESPUCCI

VASCO DE BALBOA VASCO DE BALBOA VASCO DE BALBOA VASCO DE BALBOA VASCO DE BALBOA

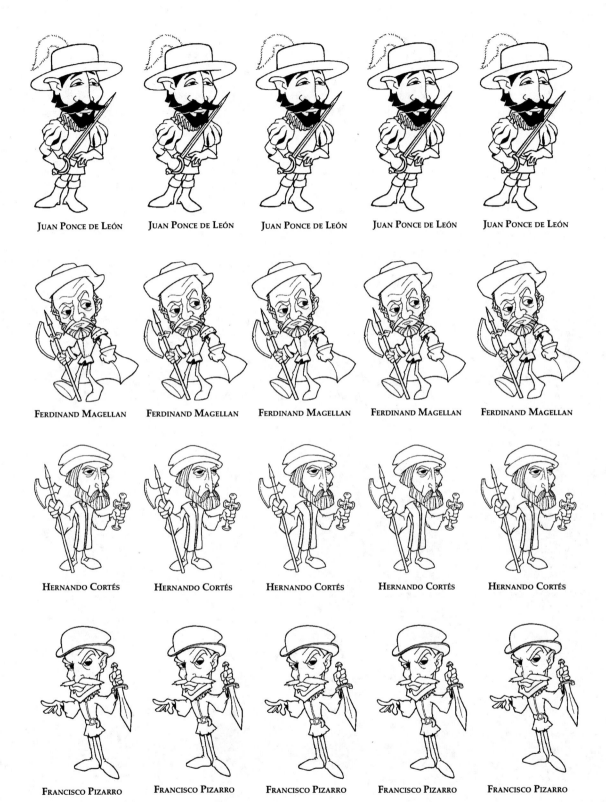

JUAN PONCE DE LEÓN   JUAN PONCE DE LEÓN   JUAN PONCE DE LEÓN   JUAN PONCE DE LEÓN   JUAN PONCE DE LEÓN

FERDINAND MAGELLAN   FERDINAND MAGELLAN   FERDINAND MAGELLAN   FERDINAND MAGELLAN   FERDINAND MAGELLAN

HERNANDO CORTÉS   HERNANDO CORTÉS   HERNANDO CORTÉS   HERNANDO CORTÉS   HERNANDO CORTÉS

FRANCISCO PIZARRO   FRANCISCO PIZARRO   FRANCISCO PIZARRO   FRANCISCO PIZARRO   FRANCISCO PIZARRO

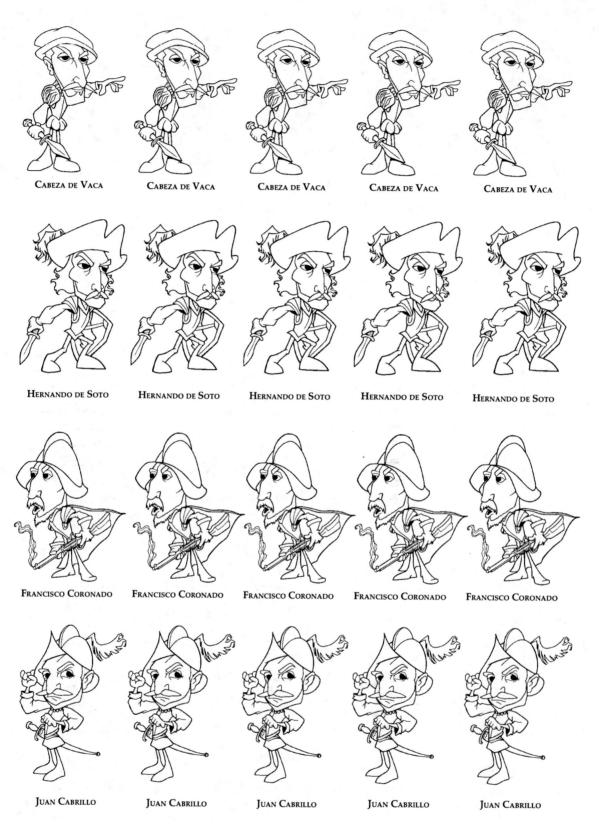

CABEZA DE VACA   CABEZA DE VACA   CABEZA DE VACA   CABEZA DE VACA   CABEZA DE VACA

HERNANDO DE SOTO   HERNANDO DE SOTO   HERNANDO DE SOTO   HERNANDO DE SOTO   HERNANDO DE SOTO

FRANCISCO CORONADO   FRANCISCO CORONADO   FRANCISCO CORONADO   FRANCISCO CORONADO   FRANCISCO CORONADO

JUAN CABRILLO   JUAN CABRILLO   JUAN CABRILLO   JUAN CABRILLO   JUAN CABRILLO

THE FUTURE OF NEW SPAIN

By 1545, Spain had claimed huge areas of land in North America and South America. Beginning in 1498, during his third voyage to the New World, Christopher Columbus claimed the mainland of South America for Spain. This led to South America's first permanent settlements and Balboa's discovery of the Pacific Ocean.

In 1513, Juan Ponce (PON•say) de León claimed all of Florida for Spain. By 1530, Spanish conquistadors (con•KEE•stah•dorz) Francisco Pizarro (puh•ZAR•roh) and Hernando Cortés had defeated the Aztec and Inca empires. The newly claimed land became known as New Spain. The victories of Cortés and Pizarro gave Spain complete control of Mexico.

In 1527, Spanish explorer Cabeza (cah•VAY•thah) de Vaca (thay•VAH•cah) sailed from Spain on an expedition to build colonies in North America. Hurricanes destroyed his ships. De Vaca spent eight years wandering through the deserts of Arizona and New Mexico. When he finally reached Mexico City in New Spain, Cabeza de Vaca told wild stories of golden cities in present-day New Mexico. This sent groups of gold seekers led by Francisco Coronado and Juan Cabrillo (cah•BREE•yo) in search of what the Spanish called the Seven Cities of Gold. Land throughout the present-day Southwest region of the United States was claimed for Spain.

Meanwhile, Hernando de Soto spent two years searching for a water route to Asia. During his journey, de Soto claimed most of the land in the present-day Southeast region of the United States for Spain.

SPANISH MISSIONS

Spain knew that the only way to take complete control of its new empire was to build permanent settlements. Settlers were needed to **defend** Spain's territory against other countries that might want to take it from them. Thousands of Native Americans lived in Spain's newly claimed land. The Spanish government decided to use the Native Americans to protect New Spain.

In 1565, Catholic priests built the first successful mission in St. Augustine, Florida. Other priests were sent to establish mission villages among the Native Americans in the present-day states of Arizona, California, Colorado, New Mexico, and Texas. The priests were told to teach the Native Americans about the Catholic religion and prepare them for Spanish control.

Spain's rulers wanted the Native Americans in New Spain to give up their native customs and become **allies** with Spain. The Spanish government hoped that the Native Americans would help fight if Spain ever went to war with another country. Building missions and training an army of Native Americans would give Spain a firm hold on its huge territory.

BUILDING MISSION VILLAGES

Getting the Native Americans to come to the missions was not easy. The Spanish priests gave them gifts of glass beads, clothing, blankets, and food. The priests gained the trust of some of the Native Americans who agreed to move inside of the mission villages. Native Americans who were not willing to come to the missions were kidnapped by Spanish soldiers. The soldiers treated the Native Americans badly, often beating them. Once they were inside of the mission villages, the Native Americans were not allowed to leave.

MISSION LIFE

More than 150 Spanish missions were established in North America. The goal at the mission villages was to teach the Native Americans about Spanish customs and develop them into hard working Spanish citizens. The men were taught how to raise livestock and grow crops of corn, beans, squash, and cotton. Other skills included leather **tanning**, brick making, **blacksmithing**, and **construction**. Women learned how to cook, sew, spin wool, and weave.

Religion classes were taught. The Native Americans were expected to attend church services several times each day. They were not permitted to practice their native customs, speak their native languages, or celebrate their religious ceremonies. Those who broke the rules or tried to escape from the missions were severely punished before being forced to return.

SUCCESS AND FAILURE

Some of the Spanish missions were very successful. In Arizona, for example, many of the Native Americans welcomed the Spanish priests. They were eager to learn how to grow crops in Arizona's hot, dry desert. In Texas, hungry Native Americans were willing to trade hard work for plenty of food and protection from enemy tribes.

MISSIONARY PRIEST

In Colorado, California, and New Mexico, many of the missions were not very successful. Colorado's Native Americans were hunters who traveled from place to place in search of buffalo and deer. Building missions among Native Americans who were always moving was difficult. In California, the Native American groups who lived along the Pacific Coast were hunters and gatherers who enjoyed plenty of food, wealth, and open spaces. They were not willing to help Spain with its plan.

In the 1650s, a **drought** struck New Mexico. Crops died and hundreds of Native Americans starved to death. The Pueblo people blamed the Spanish missionaries because they were not permitted to perform their rainmaking ceremonies. The Pueblo **revolted** and burned down the mission villages. Spanish priests and more than 1,000 Spanish colonists were killed.

ENGLAND AND FRANCE

While Spain built missions in the Southwest, English settlers built colonies in the East. By the 1680s, England had established 12 of its 13 original colonies along the Atlantic Coast.

In 1682, French explorer Robert La Salle sailed down the Mississippi River and claimed all of the land around the river for France. In honor of King Louis XIV, La Salle named the entire region Louisiana. Louisiana was a huge area of **New France** that **extended** east to west from the Appalachian (ap•uh•LAY•shun) Mountains to the Rocky Mountains. From north to south, Louisiana stretched from the Great Lakes to the Gulf of Mexico.

Some of the land in Louisiana had been claimed for Spain by Hernando de Soto. Unfortunately, Spain had not built any permanent settlements in this area and France easily claimed Louisiana for itself.

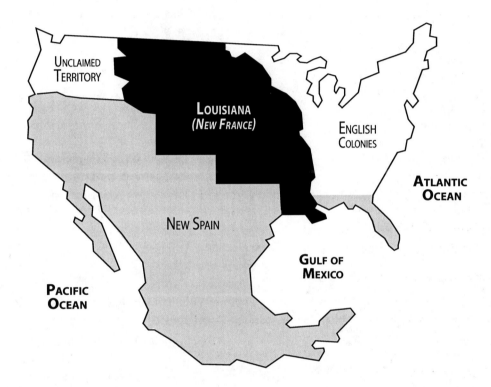

THE END OF NEW SPAIN

In the early 1800s, the Spanish empire began having problems. The Mexican citizens who lived in New Spain wanted freedom from the Spanish government. They were tired of being told what to do by a government in Spain that was thousands of miles away. One by one, Spain's colonies fought for **independence**. In 1821, Mexico declared its complete independence from Spain. The Mexican government took control of New Spain and all of its missions.

Spanish control over North and South America and the Native Americans had ended. Land and people that had been conquered by Spanish conquistadors now belonged to Mexico. Spain had been in control for more than 300 years. In less than 25 years, the United States would declare war on Mexico and take control of most of Mexico's land for itself.

≋≋≋ THE FUTURE OF NEW SPAIN ≋≋≋

Directions: Read each question carefully. Darken the circle for the correct answer.

1 **Which explorer claimed the mainland of South America for Spain?**

   A Hernando de Soto

   B Cabeza de Vaca

   C Christopher Columbus

   D Juan Cabrillo

2 **Which explorer claimed Florida for Spain?**

   F Christopher Columbus

   G Juan Ponce de León

   H Francisco Pizarro

   J Hernando de Soto

3 **Which explorers defeated the Aztec and Inca empires?**

   A Pizarro and Cortés

   B Columbus and Pizarro

   C Cortés and de Soto

   D De Vaca and de Soto

4 **After reading about the Spanish missions, you learn that –**

   F Spain planned to use the missions to protect its land in New Spain

   G priests were sent to remove all of the Native Americans from Spain's newly claimed land

   H Spain's leaders wanted the Native Americans to teach the priests about their native customs

   J the first successful Spanish mission was built in New Mexico

5 **Which statement about mission life is false?**

   A Religion classes were taught.

   B Native Americans left when they wanted.

   C The men were taught to raise livestock and grow crops.

   D Those who broke the rules were severely punished.

6 **Why weren't Spanish missions in Colorado very successful?**

   F The Native Americans in Colorado lived along the Pacific Coast and enjoyed plenty of food, wealth, and open spaces.

   G There weren't any Native Americans living in Colorado.

   H The Native Americans in Colorado were hunters who moved from place to place.

   J A drought struck Colorado and the Native Americans blamed the Spanish missionaries.

7 **What can you learn from studying the map on the last page?**

   A Louisiana was west of the English Colonies.

   B New Spain was east of the Gulf of Mexico.

   C New Spain was north of Louisiana.

   D The English Colonies bordered the Pacific Ocean.

READING

Answers

1 Ⓐ Ⓑ ⓒ Ⓓ   5 Ⓐ Ⓑ ⓒ Ⓓ

2 Ⓕ Ⓖ Ⓗ Ⓙ   6 Ⓕ Ⓖ Ⓗ Ⓙ

3 Ⓐ Ⓑ ⓒ Ⓓ   7 Ⓐ Ⓑ ⓒ Ⓓ

4 Ⓕ Ⓖ Ⓗ Ⓙ

LET'S TALK ABOUT SPANISH MISSIONS

The arrival of Spanish missionaries and soldiers into New Spain forever changed the lives of the area's Native Americans. Read the questions below about the Spanish missions and write your answers on the lines provided. Use the back of this paper if you need more room. Be ready to discuss some of your answers.

- **Thousands of Native Americans lived in New Spain before the arrival of Spanish missionaries and soldiers.**

  If you had been a child living in a Native American village, how would you have felt about the arrival of the Spanish missionaries and soldiers? What right did your family have to keep the Spanish soldiers from entering your village?

  _____

  _____

  If you had been a child of a Spanish missionary or soldier, how would you have felt about living in New Spain? What right did your family have to enter the Native American villages and kidnap their families?

  _____

  _____

- **While living at the missions, the Native Americans were forced to work long hours in the fields and give up their Native American languages and customs.**

  Why do you think the Spanish missionaries and soldiers were able to force the Native Americans to work in the fields and give up their languages and customs? If you had been a Native American, what could you have done to change this situation?

  _____

  _____

  What rules and laws do we have in America that would keep this sort of thing from happening today?

  _____

  _____

～～～～ VOCABULARY QUIZ ～～～～

SPANISH EXPLORERS AND CONQUISTADORS
PART V

Directions: Match the vocabulary word on the left with its definition on the right. Put the letter for the definition on the blank next to the vocabulary word it matches. Use each word and definition only once.

1. _____ ambushed

2. _____ artifacts

3. _____ crossbows

4. _____ allies

5. _____ brutality

6. _____ exhibits

7. _____ exported

8. _____ blacksmithing

9. _____ engineers

10. _____ habitats

11. _____ gangrene

12. _____ construction

13. _____ Great Lakes

14. _____ hoax

15. _____ harbor

16. _____ defend

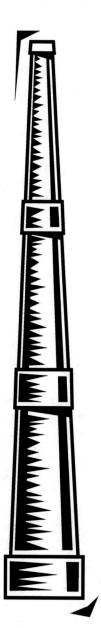

A.   high powered weapons that shoot arrows by pulling a trigger.

B.   French colonies in North America from 1534 to 1763.

C.   heating and hammering iron into different shapes.

D.   the piece of land that separates the Caribbean Sea from the Gulf of Mexico.

E.   long period of time with no rain.

F.   animals raised on a farm to eat or sell for profit.

G.   the elected official in charge of money.

H.   early settlers who prepared the way for others to follow.

I.   sheltered area of water deep enough to provide ships a place to anchor.

J.   fought against people in charge.

K.   objects and tools used by early humans for eating, cooking, and hunting.

L.   the process of soaking animal hides in a solution to turn them into leather.

M.   groups of people who come together to help one another in times of trouble.

N.   to examine carefully.

17. _____ panhandle

18. _____ investigate

19. _____ legacy

20. _____ drought

21. _____ Yucatán Peninsula

22. _____ observatory

23. _____ extended

24. _____ pioneers

25. _____ independence

26. _____ pueblo

27. _____ livestock

28. _____ New France

29. _____ rebellion

30. _____ treasurer

31. _____ revolted

32. _____ tanning

O. scientists who are skilled at building mines, ships, buildings, bridges, and chemical plants.

P. five large lakes located in North America at the border between Canada and the United States. The names of the lakes are Superior, Michigan, Huron, Erie, and Ontario.

Q. death of a body part due to lack of blood supply.

R. to keep safe from danger, attack, or harm.

S. a place that has instruments for looking at stars and planets.

T. extreme cruelty.

U. the act of disobeying authority.

V. sent items out of the country for sale or trade.

W. a type of Native American village.

X. a trick.

Y. a narrow piece of land that sticks out.

Z. something left after one dies.

AA. places where plants and animals grow or live in nature.

BB. stretched.

CC. attacked by surprise.

DD. not being under the control or rule of someone else.

EE. work that involves putting something together.

FF. displays.

GLOSSARY

a•ban•doned gave up completely.

ac•cused blamed or charged with a crime.

a•do•be a heavy clay used for making bricks.

ag•ri•cul•ture planting crops and raising farm animals.

al•lies groups of people who come together to help one another in times of trouble.

am•bushed attacked by surprise.

an•chor secure a boat so it won't float away.

ap•point•ed chosen or selected.

ar•chae•ol•o•gists scientists who study past human life by looking at prehistoric fossils and tools.

ar•chi•tects people who design buildings.

ar•ti•facts objects and tools used by early humans for eating, cooking, and hunting.

ar•ti•sans people who are skilled at making things.

A•sia the world's largest continent with more than half of the Earth's population.

au•to•bi•og•ra•phy the story of your life written by you.

Bar•ba•ry Coast the coast of the Mediterranean Sea where pirates went for protection.

bar•ri•er is•land a long sandy island that runs next to a shore and provides protection from hurricanes and tidal waves.

bays bodies of water surrounded by land that open to the sea.

be•friend•ed made friends with someone.

be•head•ed cut off someone's head.

black•smith•ing heating and hammering iron into different shapes.

bi•og•ra•phies stories of a person's life written by someone else.

block•ade shutting off a place to keep people and supplies from coming in or going out.

bru•tal•i•ty extreme cruelty.

can•als waterways that bring water to crops.

cap•i•tal the city that serves as the center of government for the state or nation.

cap•tives people who are held without permission.

Ca•rib•be•an Sea an arm of the Atlantic Ocean surrounded on the north and east by the West Indies, on the south by South America, and on the west by Central America.

ca•the•dral a large important church, usually the church of a bishop.

cer•e•mo•nies religious or spiritual gatherings.

chan•nel a long, narrow, deep part of a body of water.

Chris•ti•an•i•ty a religion based on the life and teachings of Jesus Christ.

cit•i•zen person in a city, town, state, or country who enjoys the freedom to vote and participate in government decisions.

cloves spices made from the dried flower buds of an evergreen tree.

coast an area of land that borders water.

col•o•ny a settlement of people who are ruled by another country.

com•pan•ions friends.

con•flicts struggles or disagreements.

con•quered defeated by force.

con•quis•ta•dor a Spanish soldier who conquered the Native Americans of Mexico and Peru.

con•struc•tion work that involves putting something together.

con•ti•nent one of seven large areas of land on the globe.

con•vinced talked someone into doing something your way.

cross•bows high powered weapons that shoot arrows by pulling a trigger.

cul•ture a group of people with a shared set of beliefs, goals, religious customs, attitudes, and social practices.

cur•rents quickly moving bodies of water.

cus•toms usual ways of doing things.

debt money that is owed to someone else.

de•feat•ed won victory over.

de•fend to keep safe from danger, attack, or harm.

de•nied didn't agree to.

do•min•ions large territories with one ruler.

drought long period of time with no rain.

dunes mounds of sand that pile up when the wind blows.

em•er•ald a valuable green colored stone that is often used in jewelry.

em•per•or the male ruler of an empire.

em•pire a group of territories or peoples under one ruler.

en•dan•gered in danger of disappearing forever.

en•gi•neers scientists who are skilled at building mines, ships, buildings, bridges, and chemical plants.

e•qua•tor the invisible line that cuts through the center of the Earth from east to west.

e•ro•sion destruction by wind and rain.

es•ti•mat•ed guessed.

e•ter•nal forever.

Eu•rope•an a person from Europe, the sixth smallest of Earth's seven continents.

ex•hib•its displays.

ex•iled forced to leave.

ex•pand•ing growing larger.

ex•pe•di•tions journeys for the purpose of exploring.

ex•port•ed sent items out of the country for sale or trade.

ex•tend•ed stretched.

ex•ter•nal on the outside.

fer•tile rich soil that produces a large number of crops.

fer•til•ized added a material to the soil to make crops grow better.

fleet large group of ships.

flint a very hard stone that makes a spark when struck by steel.

for•eign•ers people from another country or nation.

for•ma•tions arrangements of something.

fos•sils remains of plants or animals preserved in earth or rock.

found•ed started or established.

gan•grene death of a body part due to lack of blood supply.

ge•og•ra•phy the study of the Earth's surface.

gov•er•nor a person who is in charge of an area or group.

Great Lakes five large lakes located in North America at the border between Canada and the United States. The names of the lakes are Superior, Michigan, Huron, Erie, and Ontario.

hab•i•tats places where plants and animals grow or live in nature.

har•bor sheltered area of water deep enough to provide ships a place to anchor.

harsh very uncomfortable conditions.

har•vest pick crops.

His•pan•ic a person who was originally from Spain.

His•pan•i•o•la an island in the West Indies that lies between Cuba and Puerto Rico.

his•to•ri•ans people who study history.

hoax a trick.

hos•tile angry and unfriendly.

ig•nored didn't listen to.

im•port to bring items into a country for the purpose of selling them.

in•de•pen•dence not being under the control or rule of someone else.

in•hab•i•tants people who live or settle in a place.

in•no•cent not guilty.

in•vad•ed entered an area and took it over by force.

in•ves•ti•gate to examine carefully.

ir•ri•gate to water crops.

is•lands areas of land that are completely surrounded by water.

Isth•mus of Pan•a•ma the narrow strip of land connecting North and South America.

jour•nal a written record of daily events.

kid•napped took someone without permission.

leg•a•cy something left after one dies.

leg•end a story told over and over again throughout history that can't be proven to be true.

live•stock animals raised on a farm to eat or sell for profit.

loy•al•ly faithfully.

main•land a large piece of land set apart from an island.

maize corn.

ma•lar•i•a a disease caused by mosquitoes that spreads to other humans and results in chills and fever.

mer•chant a buyer or seller whose goal is to make money.

me•sas steep hills with flat tops.

mil•i•tar•y people who are part of the armed forces who may be asked to go to war.

mis•sion church.

mis•sion•ar•y a person sent to spread a religious faith.

mon•u•ment building, stone, or statue created to remember a person or event.

mourn to feel and express deep sadness.

Mus•lims people who follow the laws of Islam and worship God whom they call Allah.

na•tive belonging to a place because you were born there.

nav•i•ga•tion controlling the direction of a ship.

New France French colonies in North America from 1534 to 1763.

New Spain Spanish colonies that were once in parts of North, Central, and South America.

New World a term once used to describe the continents of North America and South America.

no•ble•man a man born to high rank.

North A•mer•i•ca one of seven continents in the world. Bounded by Alaska on the northwest, Greenland on the northeast, Florida on the southeast, and Mexico on the southwest.

ob•ser•va•to•ry a place that has instruments for looking at stars and planets.

of•fi•cials people with high rank who have the power to make decisions.

pan•han•dle a narrow piece of land that sticks out.

pet•ro•glyph carving or drawing in rocks usually made by people who lived a long time ago.

Phil•ip•pines a group of islands southeast of China in the Pacific Ocean.

pi•o•neers early settlers who prepared the way for others to follow.

plains wide treeless areas of land.

pleu•ri•sy pain in the lungs that causes chills, fever, and coughing.

por•ce•lain a hard white clay that is heated and glazed to make ceramic dishes.

Por•tu•gal a country along the Atlantic Ocean on the southwestern edge of Europe whose capital is Lisbon.

pre•served protected from injury or ruin so more can be learned.

prov•ince a part of a country having a government of its own.

pro•vi•sions supplies of food taken on a trip.

pueb•lo a type of Native American village.

quar•ries open pits that provide stones for building.

raid•ed entered someone's property for the purpose of stealing.

ran•som money paid for the safe return of a person who has been taken without permission.

re•bel•lion the act of disobeying authority.

re•cruit to find people who are willing to join a military force.

re•sourc•es things found in nature that are valuable to humans.

re•spect to honor someone.

re•volt•ed fought against people in charge.

sac•ri•ficed killed an animal or human being as a spiritual offering.

schol•ar a well educated person who is a specialist on a subject.

sculp•tures figures or designs shaped out of clay, marble, or metal.

scur•vy a disease caused from lack of vitamin C that results in swollen and bleeding gums, bleeding under the skin, and extreme weakness.

sea•port a sheltered area where ships can load and unload supplies.

shal•low a hole that is not very deep.

spe•cies groups of plants or animals that are alike in many ways.

Spice Is•lands a group of islands in Indonesia, a nation in southeast Asia.

strait a narrow strip of sea between two pieces of land.

strand•ed left alone without any help.

tan•ning the process of soaking animal hides in a solution to turn them into leather.

tav•ern a public place that sells alcoholic beverages.

tex•tiles fabrics made from weaving or knitting yarn.

tor•ture to cause severe physical or mental pain to someone.

tour•ist a person who travels for pleasure.

trea•son a crime against your country's government.

treas•ur•er the elected official in charge of money.

tur•quoise a bluish green stone that turns bright blue when polished.

voy•age journey that is usually made by water.

West In•dies a chain of islands in the Caribbean Sea that stretches from the southern tip of Florida to the northeastern corner of South America.

wit•ness•es people who are called upon to tell the truth about what they heard or saw.

wor•shipped honored someone; usually during a religious ceremony.

Yu•ca•tán Pen•in•su•la the piece of land that separates the Caribbean Sea from the Gulf of Mexico.

ANSWERS

ANSWERS TO COMPREHENSION QUESTIONS

CHRISTOPHER COLUMBUS

1. C
2. H
3. A
4. F
5. D
6. G
7. C

AMERIGO VESPUCCI

1. D
2. G
3. C
4. J
5. A
6. J
7. C

VASCO NUÑEZ DE BALBOA

1. C
2. F
3. D
4. H
5. A
6. H
7. B
8. F

PONCE DE LEÓN

1. A
2. J
3. B
4. J
5. C
6. F
7. B
8. J

FERDINAND MAGELLAN

1. B
2. F
3. B
4. G
5. D
6. F

HERNANDO CORTÉS

1. A
2. J
3. B
4. G
5. C
6. F
7. C

FRANCISCO PIZARRO

1. C
2. G
3. D
4. G
5. C
6. G
7. A

CABEZA DE VACA

1. C
2. F
3. D
4. H
5. C
6. J
7. B
8. G

HERNANDO DE SOTO

1. C
2. G
3. C
4. F
5. D
6. F
7. D

FRANCISCO DE CORONADO

1. D
2. H
3. C
4. H
5. A
6. J
7. B
8. J

JUAN CABRILLO

1. C
2. J
3. B
4. H
5. D
6. F
7. C
8. H
9. B

THE FUTURE OF NEW SPAIN

1. C
2. G
3. A
4. F
5. B
6. H
7. A

ANSWERS TO VOCABULARY QUIZZES

PART I	PART II	PART III	PART IV	PART V
1. E	1. Z	1. K	1. NN	1. CC
2. W	2. D	2. W	2. T	2. K
3. M	3. M	3. D	3. A	3. A
4. B	4. N	4. M	4. M	4. M
5. O	5. I	5. BB	5. KK	5. T
6. EE	6. R	6. Y	6. F	6. FF
7. H	7. A	7. Q	7. I	7. V
8. CC	8. U	8. T	8. EE	8. C
9. HH	9. BB	9. G	9. W	9. O
10. F	10. T	10. FF	10. N	10. AA
11. Y	11. F	11. J	11. II	11. Q
12. A	12. W	12. R	12. X	12. EE
13. U	13. B	13. N	13. G	13. P
14. II	14. CC	14. E	14. D	14. X
15. I	15. S	15. Z	15. BB	15. I
16. Q	16. K	16. DD	16. JJ	16. R
17. N	17. H	17. H	17. O	17. Y
18. AA	18. Y	18. O	18. DD	18. N
19. K	19. O	19. L	19. R	19. Z
20. P	20. AA	20. CC	20. B	20. E
21. V	21. E	21. I	21. P	21. D
22. GG	22. X	22. U	22. MM	22. S
23. T	23. Q	23. F	23. S	23. BB
24. L	24. C	24. X	24. J	24. H
25. JJ	25. L	25. P	25. Z	25. DD
26. Z	26. G	26. C	26. C	26. W
27. D	27. V	27. S	27. FF	27. F
28. S	28. J	28. AA	28. U	28. B
29. BB	29. P	29. B	29. CC	29. U
30. FF		30. V	30. LL	30. G
31. R		31. EE	31. V	31. J
32. DD		32. A	32. H	32. L
33. C			33. Y	
34. J			34. L	
35. X			35. GG	
36. G			36. Q	
			37. AA	
			38. E	
			39. HH	
			40. K	

ANSWERS TO COLUMBUS MAPPING ACTIVITY

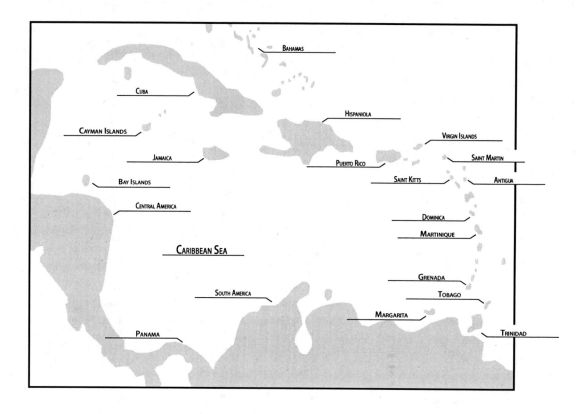

ANSWERS TO CONSIDER THE SOURCE

1. P
2. P
3. P
4. S
5. S
6. P
7. P

ANSWER TO GRID MATH

GRADING CHART FOR CONQUISTADOR STORY

CRITERIA	POINTS POSSIBLE	POINTS EARNED
Answered each of 5 prewriting Questions	**50** (10 points per question)	
Spelling/Grammar	**20**	
Neatness of Final Draft	**15**	
Orally Reading Story	**15**	
TOTAL	**100**	

GRADING CHART FOR JOURNAL WRITING

CRITERIA	POINTS POSSIBLE	POINTS EARNED
Clearly describes content of overheard conversations	20	
Decribes how conversations make him or her feel	20	
States whether or not friends will be told about overheard conversations	5	
Describes what strange men are planning to do	20	
Describes what will happen to self, village, and family	20	
Gives other details that make the journal entry interesting	15	
TOTAL	100	

ANSWERS TO CARDINAL/INTERMEDIATE DIRECTIONS MAPPING

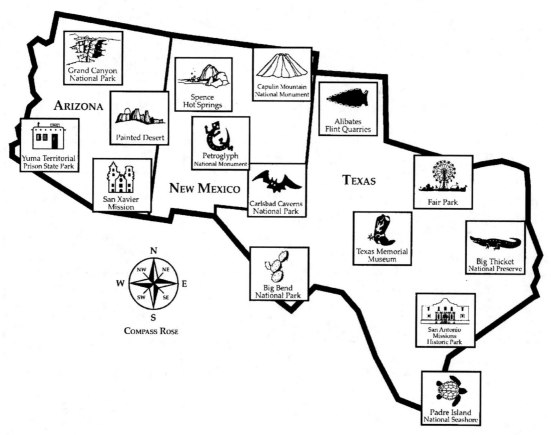

ANSWERS TO HERNANDO DE SOTO TIME TRAVEL

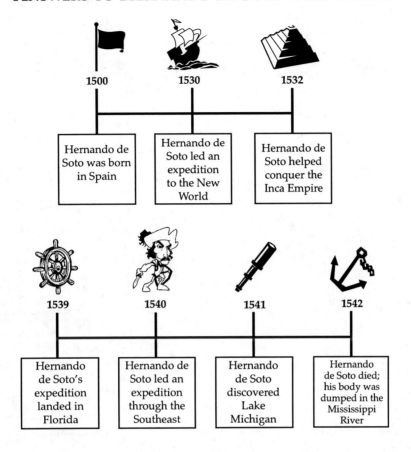

1500

Hernando de Soto was born in Spain

1530

Hernando de Soto led an expedition to the New World

1532

Hernando de Soto helped conquer the Inca Empire

1539

Hernando de Soto's expedition landed in Florida

1540

Hernando de Soto led an expedition through the Southeast

1541

Hernando de Soto discovered Lake Michigan

1542

Hernando de Soto died; his body was dumped in the Mississippi River

ANSWERS TO LATITUDE/LONGITUDE MAPPING

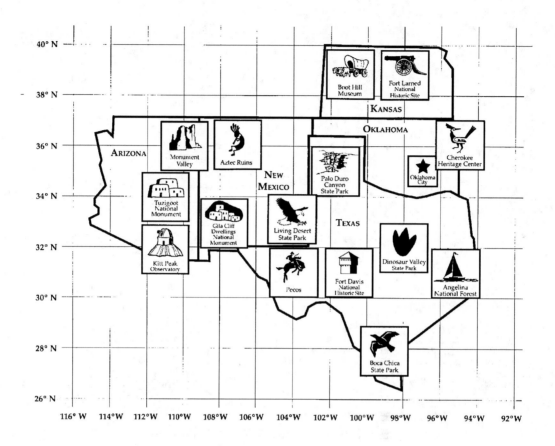

GRADING CHART FOR FIND THE FIB

CRITERIA	POINTS POSSIBLE	POINTS EARNED
Fifteen True Facts	**60** (4 pts. each)	
Five False Facts	**20** (4 pts. each)	
Spelling/Grammar	10	
Neatness	5	
Answer Sheet	5	
TOTAL	**100**	

BIBLIOGRAPHY

Bartleby: 'American Heritage Dictionary of the English Language: Fourth Edition' 2000
[Online] Available <http://www.bartleby.com> (August 1, 2008)

Carson, Robert. The World's Great Explorers: Hernando de Soto. Chicago:
Children's Press, 1991.

CarpeNoctem: 'Hernando Cortés: Spanish Conquerer' 2003 [Online] Available
<http://www.carpenoctem.tv/military/cortes.html> (June 3, 2008)

Covey, Cyclone: 'Cabeza de Vaca's Adventures in the Unknown Interior of America' 1961
[Online] Available <http://www.eldritchpress.org/cdv/rel.htm> (March 2, 2008)

Desert USA: 'Francisco Vázquez de Coronado' 2008 [Online] Available
<http://www.desertusa.com/mag98/sep/papr/coronado.html> (July 5, 2008)

Enchanted Learning: 'Christopher Columbus: Explorer' 2008 [Online] Available
<http://www.enchantedlearning.com/explorers/page/c/columbus.shtml>
(August 6, 2008)

Enchanted Learning: 'Juan Ponce de Leon: Explorer' 2008 [Online] Available
<http://www.enchantedlearning.com/explorers/page/d/deleon.shtml>
(August 6, 2008)

Engels, Andre: 'Juan Ponce de León' 2005 [Online] Available
<http://www.win.tue.nl/~engels/discovery/ponce.html> (January 3, 2009)

Florida Center for Instructional Technology: 'Ponce de León: Florida's First Spanish Explorer'
2002 [Online] Available (November 3, 2008)

Grolier Online: 'Spanish Missions in U.S. History' 2008 [Online] Available
<http://www2.scholastic.com/browse/article.jsp?id=5032> (May 7, 2008)

Harmon, Dan. Juan Ponce de Leon and the Search for the Fountain of Youth. Philadelphia:
Chelsea House, 2000.

Headley, Amy and Smith, Victoria. Do American History! Glendale, Arizona: Splash!
Publications, 2003.

Headley, Amy and Smith, Victoria. Do Arizona! Glendale, Arizona: Splash! Publications, 2006.

Headley, Amy and Smith, Victoria. Do California! Glendale, Arizona: Splash! Publications,
2005.

Headley, Amy and Smith, Victoria. Do Colorado! Glendale, Arizona: Splash! Publications,
2004.

Headley, Amy and Smith, Victoria. Do Nevada! Glendale, Arizona: Splash! Publications,
2007.

Headley, Amy and Smith, Victoria. Do New Mexico! Glendale, Arizona: Splash!
Publications, 2004.

Headley, Amy and Smith, Victoria. Do Texas! Glendale, Arizona: Splash!
Publications, 2006.

Heart of San Antonio: 'The Missions' [Online] Available <http://hotx.com/missions/>
(July 1, 2008)

Heinrichs, Ann. <u>California: America the Beautiful</u>. New York: Children's Press, 1999.

Heinrichs, Ann. <u>Florida: America the Beautiful</u>. New York: Children's Press, 1998.

Heinrichs, Ann. <u>Texas: America the Beautiful</u>. New York: Children's Press, 1999.

Kent, Zachary. <u>Kansas: America the Beautiful</u>. Chicago: Children's Press, 1991

Knight, Kevin: 'Amerigo Vespucci' 2008 [Online] Available
<http://www.newadvent.org/cathen/15384b.htm> (December 10, 2008)

Koeller, David: 'Coronado Explorers what will become the Southwestern United States' 2003 [Online] Available <http://www.thenagain.info/WebChron/NorthAmerica/Coronado.html> (April 10, 2008)

Lexico Publishing Group: 'Dictionary.com' 2004 [Online]
Available <http:// dictionary.reference.com/> (September 1, 2008)

EMuseum@Minnesota State University Mankato: 'Inca' 2007 [Online] Available
<http://www.mnsu.edu/emuseum/prehistory/latinamerica/south/cultures/inca.html> (September 21, 2008)

Moran, Patrick Gerard: 'Texas Missions' [Online] Available
<http://users.ev1.net/~gpmoran/txmsns.htm> (April 10, 2008)

National Park Service: 'San Antonio Missions' 2006 [Online] Available
<http://www.nps.gov/saan/> (January 7, 2009)

Pickering, Keith A: 'The Columbus Navigation Homepage' 1997 [Online] Available
<http://www.columbusnavigation.com/> (June 2, 2008)

Rosenberg, Matt: 'Amerigo Vespucci' 2007 [Online] Available
<http://geography.about.com/cs/historicalgeog/a/amerigo.htm> (July 2, 2008)

San Diego Historical Society: 'San Diego Biographies: Juan Rodriguez Cabrillo' 2001 [Online] Available <http://www.sandiegohistory.org/bio/cabrillo/cabrillo.htm> (February 8, 2008)

Sheppard, Donald: 'Spanish Exploration and Conquest of Native America' [Online] Available
<http://www.floridahistory.com/> (November 13, 2008)

Sherwood Elementary School: 'Explorers of the Millennium' 1998 [Online] Available
<http://library.thinkquest.org/4034/> (July 12, 2008)

Steins, Richard. <u>Exploration and Settlement</u>. Texas: Steck-Vaughn, 2000.

Studyworld: 'Amerigo Vespucci' 2008 [Online] Available
<http://www.studyworld.com/Amerigo_Vespucci.htm> (April 10, 2008)

The Texas State Historical Association: 'The Handbook of Texas Online' 2003 [Online]
Available <http://www.tsha.utexas.edu/handbook/online/index.html> (August 8, 2008)

The West Film Project: 'Alvar Nuñez Cabeza de Vaca' 2001 [Online] Available
<http://www.pbs.org/weta/thewest/people/a_c/cabezadevaca.htm> (January 3, 2009)

University of Calgary: 'The Conquest of the Aztec Empire' 1997 [Online] Available
<http://www.ucalgary.ca/applied_history/tutor/eurvoya/aztec.html> (May 3, 2008)

Wood, Michael: 'Conquistadors' [Online] Available
<http://www.pbs.org/conquistadors/index.html> (June 9, 2008)

Woods, Mario. <u>The World of Native Americans</u>. New York: Peter Bedrick Books, 1997.